Simply
Smoothies

200 Refreshing Drinks
for Life, Health, and Fun

by Delia Quigley

Adams Media
Avon, Massachusetts

Copyright ©2004 by Delia Quigley.
All rights reserved. This book, or parts thereof, may not be reproduced in any
form without permission from the publisher; exceptions are made for brief
excerpts used in published reviews.

Published by
Adams Media, an F+W Publications Company
57 Littlefield Street, Avon, MA 02322. U.S.A.
www.adamsmedia.com

ISBN: 1-59337-016-4

Printed in Canada.

J   I   H   G   F   E   D   C   B

Library of Congress Cataloging-in-Publication Data
Quigley, Delia.
Simply smoothies / Delia Quigley.
p.   cm.
ISBN 1-59337-016-4
1. Blenders (Cookery) 2. Smoothies (Beverages) I. Title.
TX840.B5.Q54 2004
641.8'75–dc22
2003019614

This publication is designed to provide accurate and authoritative information with regard to
the subject matter covered. It is sold with the understanding that the publisher is not engaged
in rendering legal, accounting, or other professional advice. If legal advice or other expert
assistance is required, the services of a competent professional person should be sought.
   —From a *Declaration of Principles* jointly adopted by a Committee of the American Bar
            Association and a Committee of Publishers and Associations

This publication is designed to provide accurate and authoritative information with
regard to the subject matter covered. It is sold with the understanding that the
publisher is not engaged in rendering professional medical advice. If assistance is
required, the services of a competent professional person should be sought.

Many of the designations used by manufacturers and sellers to distinguish their
products are claimed as trademarks. Where those designations appear in this book and
Adams Media was aware of a trademark claim, the designations have been printed in
initial capital letters.

Cover photo © Shipes Shooter/Stock Food
Interior photographs © PhotoDisc, Inc.

This book is available at quantity discounts for bulk purchases.
For information, call 1-800-872-5627.

Contents

Introduction

When I was growing up, my favorite drink was a milk shake, vanilla, thick and creamy, from the local soda shop. My brothers loved chocolate, and none of us would even consider a strawberry milk shake. Fruit in a shake? No way! The closest we came was a banana split or ice cream sundae, and the idea of a fruit smoothie was a completely foreign concept. However, today I start my morning with a jazzed-up smoothie and won't even consider having a milk shake because of the sugar, high dairy fat, and calories.

Smoothies are the milk shake of the new millennium, where feeding the brain, body, and spirit are at the forefront of our minds. Good for you and delicious, they can be prepared to meet your daily vitamin requirements, satisfy a quarrelsome sweet tooth, and replace a meal when you're on the go.

In today's fast-paced world, where getting a healthy meal on the table for yourself and your family is a huge challenge, a few high-quality ingredients tossed into a blender can prove to be a filling, tasty, and nutritious solution. By combining the proper amounts of protein, carbohydrates, and fats, smoothies can be a filling meal packed with vitamins and minerals. As a snack, smoothies are a quick answer to low energy and hunger pangs and will hold you until you sit down later to a balanced meal.

Perhaps the greatest thing about smoothies is the endless possibilities. The sky is the limit! With so many combinations, there is surely a smoothie for every taste and lifestyle. For example, the Banana Strawberry Protein Smoothie makes a fabulous breakfast, and the Vegetable Protein Smoothie is a filling lunchtime meal.

Satisfaction to both the taste buds and the body's needs is the key here, and smoothies fit the bill on all counts. In *Simply Smoothies,* you will find 200 recipes that will take you through the year with very few repetitions of the same blend of ingredients. You'll find recipes for Healing Smoothies that can help to cleanse and heal the body or prevent illness. You'll also find smoothies for those throw-caution-to-the-wind times when only something decadent and rich will satisfy your sweet tooth. In addition to all the fun and creative recipes, you will find a chart of ingredients at the end of the book that will awaken your creativity and imagination and show you how to create your own smoothie recipes.

Once you familiarize yourself with the nutritional information in Chapter 1 on fruits and vegetables, you can be sure that you are receiving your proper allotment of nutrients when drinking your daily smoothie. This book will be your step-by-step guide to the art of making the perfect smoothie, from juice to nuts to proper equipment.

Keeping a variety of ingredients on hand, such as frozen organic berries, flax seeds, juice concentrates, high-quality oils, and meal powders, allows you to whip up your favorite smoothie in a pinch. Be sure to keep plenty of fresh fruit and vegetables on hand, ripening bananas on the counter, and a variety of nuts and seeds stored in jars so you'll have numerous options to experiment with in creating new taste sensations. In the freezer, ice cubes or frozen juice cubes come in handy to help chill a creation and give it a thick, creamy consistency. Use your imagination and trust your taste buds to tell you what they like, or try any of the recipes in *Simply Smoothies* and enjoy a truly delightful experience.

Chapter 1

In the Pantry

It is early morning and you're in a hurry to get yourself and your family together and out the door to work and school. While your choice for a quick-fix breakfast may be a bowl of sugar-coated, refined-grain cereal with low-fat milk for the kids and the usual bagel with a smear of cream cheese or butter for you, this morning's jump-start fades fast, followed by the inevitable energy crash around midmorning. You vow again to improve your diet and eat more healthful foods, but you're also not sure what that means or what foods you should have on hand to prepare quick meals. Enter, the smoothie: With a full array of fresh fruits and vegetables, juices and milks, you can create a substantial meal or pick-me-up throughout the day, a perfect solution to your quick meal dilemma.

Before you start your blenders, let's begin with a list of ingredients you should have available in the refrigerator or on pantry shelves so that at a moment's notice you, or your children, can whip up a delicious meal in a glass. A smoothie made with fresh fruits and vegetables lets you drink your vitamins and minerals rather than swallow them in pill form. Naturally, the smoothie goes

1

Ideally, your blood should be alkaline with a pH of 7.365. Fruits and vegetables are alkaline-forming foods for the blood and should make up the largest part of your diet.

down much easier and tastes fantastic! Take a few moments to read about the nutrient-dense foods below in order to understand their importance in your daily diet and how you can use them to create delicious smoothies.

Fruits for Your Smoothie

Fruits are most commonly used in smoothies for their sweet taste, high vitamin content, and digestible fiber. Knowing the benefits of each fruit allows you to design your daily tonic with an eye toward receiving the nutrition you will need for each day. Using a different combination of fruits in each smoothie will allow for a broader spectrum of vitamins and minerals in your diet and prevent your taste buds from becoming bored.

When choosing your fruits, make sure to buy fresh, ripe fruit in season for the highest nutrient content. When available, buy fruits that have been organically grown, as the chemicals used in industrial agriculture are known to be a possible cause of cancer. Washing fruits that have been sprayed with pesticides and herbicides does not remove the poisons because they are known to grow into the flesh of the fruit. However, since organic produce may not be readily available in your local markets, you may want to use detergent sprays available in food stores to help wash off the wax and chemicals from the outside of the fruit and vegetables.

Frozen organic fruits are available in the freezer section of your local health food store and many supermarkets. Keeping a variety of packaged frozen organic berries in your freezer prepares you for making healthy smoothies at a moment's notice. However, when fruits come into season during the summer months, take the time to freeze them for future use in your smoothies. This is an inexpensive way to take advantage of the bounty of ripe fruits that might go to waste otherwise. Rinse berries in water and gently dry them with a clean cloth or paper towel. Freeze berries in a single layer on a small cookie sheet, pour into freezer bags, label, and keep frozen until ready to use. For apples, pears, and peaches, wash, core, and slice into half-moon pieces or chunks and freeze. You can peel peaches by dropping them into boiling water for 30 seconds, then rinsing them under cold water. Remove the skin and slice the peach into sections that will be easy for a blender to purée.

Safe Soak

To make your own pesticide wash, add ½ cup of Clorox bleach or ½ cup of hydrogen peroxide to a sink full of water. Soak your fruits and vegetables for 10 to 15 minutes; then rinse well, dry, and store in the refrigerator.

Apples

"An apple a day keeps the doctor away," though it is now a cliché, is actually a statement to live by. A member of the rose family, apples are well known for cleansing the body's internal system. The entire fruit, including the skin and the core, is full of fiber and phytonutrients. The proof is in the fact that 1 cup of apple juice contains 15 milligrams of calcium, 22 milligrams of phosphorus, 1.5 milligrams of iron, 2 milligrams of sodium, 250 milligrams of potassium, trace amounts of some B-complex vitamins, and 2 milligrams of vitamin C. Naturally occurring food acids found abundantly in apples can help to block the formation of cancer-causing cells. Raw, organic apples; freshly pressed apple juice; and raw, unfiltered apple cider vinegar are good ways to utilize the anticancer benefits of apples.

Nature's Chemicals

Phytonutrients are plant chemicals that differ from nutrients such as vitamins, minerals, and amino acids. Scientific research has only just begun to understand the role these nutrients play in diet and health. There are thousands of plant chemicals that do any number of things such as protecting a plant from the sun's ultraviolet rays and environmental pollution. Consuming these phytochemicals in your daily diet is essential to optimum health and well-being.

Apricots

A member of the plum family, apricots, *Prunus armeniaca,* are high in vitamin A and contain smaller amounts of potassium, calcium, vitamin C, and iron. The Hunza people, who have lived for centuries amid the mountains that border China, Pakistan, and the former Soviet Union, are admired for their excellent health despite the rigors of living under such harsh climatic conditions. They, in turn, acknowledge the humble apricot, which they consume at almost every meal in some form or other. The apricot's high vitamin A content has been recommended for strengthening eyesight and the liver and helping to heal respiratory ailments.

Avocados

Used more as a vegetable, botanically, avocado is considered to be a fruit. Each avocado provides 82 milligrams of vitamin C, 23 milligrams of calcium, 95 milligrams of phosphorus, 1.4 milligrams of iron, 1,368 milligrams of potassium, 660 IUs of vitamin A, plus niacin and sodium. A large-sized avocado contains about 190 calories, 88 percent as monounsaturated fat, and has been prized by many ancient cultures for its ability to lubricate the joints of the body and keep the skin soft and supple. Regular consumption of avocado in the diet has been shown to lower total cholesterol while maintaining high-density lipoproteins (HDL), or good cholesterol, which helps to protect against heart disease.

Bananas

Many consider the banana to be the foundation of any smoothie. Whether freshly peeled or frozen, this fruit adds a richness and delicious taste that can often times disguise the use of less tasty ingredients. One large banana provides 11 milligrams of calcium, 35 milligrams of phosphorus, 503 milligrams of potassium, 260 IUs of vitamin A, 14 milligrams of vitamin C, and 1 milligram of iron and niacin. It is considered to be an easily digested, fiber-rich food that can coat the intestines and act as an anti-inflammatory agent to support healing. Bananas are a good food to eat when suffering from acid reflux, as they help to neutralize the hydrochloric acid in the stomach.

Berries

Berries are a large group of both wild and cultivated fruits including blueberries, blackberries, strawberries, raspberries, and cranberries. This is where you find water-soluble plant chemicals known as bioflavonoids as well as a high digestible fiber content.

Blueberries

Research has shown that blueberries contain bacteria-fighting properties that help in the treatment of urinary tract infections. Their juice is good for gout, kidney

Protective Nutrients

Bioflavonoids comprise some 4,000 antioxidants found in fruits and vegetables. They are known for their ability to prevent the buildup of cholesterol in the arteries and to protect the body from cancer-causing substances.

stones, chronic diarrhea, dysentery, sore throat, eczema, psoriasis, and rashes.

Strawberries

Three-quarters of a cup of whole strawberries supplies 62 percent of an adult's daily vitamin C requirement. Strawberries contain key elements that can help to prevent stomach cancer. Known to help eliminate toxic buildup in the blood, strawberries are also considered to be excellent skin cleansers.

Blackberries

Blackberries contain at least twice as much vitamin E as most common berries, and they supply more folate. Blackberries are used to treat a number of illnesses, including anemia and excessive menstruation in women.

Raspberries

Raspberries are well known for their healing properties, and a half-cup serving of fresh raspberries provides 16 percent of the day's folate intake and 80 percent of vitamin C requirements. Raspberries contain the phytonutrient ellagic acid, which has been seen in laboratory experiments to inhibit cancer growth. They are also used in Chinese medicine to treat the liver and kidneys and cleanse the blood of toxins.

Cranberries

Acknowledged by both ancient and contemporary physicians as useful in the treatment and prevention of urinary tract infections, cranberries are antibacterial and may also help those afflicted with urinary or kidney stones. Since cranberry bogs are usually close to the sea, there is enough iodine contained within the fruit to help an underactive thyroid.

Cantaloupe

Rich in beta-carotene, half a cantaloupe provides 9,240 IUs of vitamin A, 90 milligrams of vitamin C, 38 milligrams of calcium, 44 milligrams of phosphorus, 1.1 milligrams of iron, 33 milligrams of sodium, 682 milligrams of potassium, and 1.6 milligrams of niacin. The natural sugars and enzymes present in cantaloupe help to reduce inflammation in the digestive tract.

Cherries

Cherries are helpful for cleansing the blood of toxins by stimulating the kidney, bladder, and colon to release accumulated waste matter. They have also been known to help ease swelling and inflammation from arthritis and rheumatism. One cup of unpitted cherries contains 82 calories, 32 milligrams of calcium, 28 milligrams of phosphorus, 0.6 milligrams of iron, 3 milligrams of sodium, 277 milligrams of potassium, 160 IUs of vitamin A, some B-complex vitamins, and 15 milligrams of vitamin C.

Citrus

Best grown in subtropical Mediterranean-type climates, these fruits are known for their high vitamin C content. Citrus fruits are also helpful for cleansing the blood and liver, and having some fresh citrus juice each day may help to prevent cancers of the stomach and colon. Choose fruits with bright, even color and store at room temperature.

Grapefruits

At one time, these fruits were almost as sour as lemons, but today they have been cultivated to have a higher sugar content. Yellow or ruby red, grapefruits have been used in Chinese medicine to help digestion and to stop belching. One large grapefruit contains 51 milligrams of calcium, 51 milligrams of phosphorus, 1.3 milligrams of iron, 3 milligrams of sodium, 434 milligrams of potassium, 30 IUs of vitamin A, some B-complex vitamins, and 122 milligrams of vitamin C.

Oranges

One orange supplies more than 90 percent of an adult's daily vitamin C requirement, but you want to have freshly squeezed organic juice as the pasteurization process kills off much of the nutrients. Oranges are used in Chinese medicine to help stimulate the digestive system, prevent scurvy, and strengthen the gums.

Lemons/Limes

Although lemons are high in citric acid and, consequently, somewhat tart, they are very alkaline-forming to the blood pH and are, therefore, excellent for cleansing the body of toxic sludge. To get the most juice out of your lemons, roll them on a countertop with the palm of your hand, giving just enough pressure to soften the outer skin.

Due to their high vitamin C content, limes were given to sailors to prevent scurvy on long voyages at sea. These citrus fruits also help the body to absorb iron more easily.

Dates

One of the oldest recorded fruits, dating back to the Garden of Eden, dates are prized for their taste, sweetness, and nutrient properties. Ten dates provide 47 milligrams of calcium, 50 milligrams of phosphorus, 2.4 milligrams of iron, 1 milligram of sodium, 518 milligrams of potassium, 40 IUs of vitamin A, and 1.8 milligrams of niacin.

Figs

Loaded with iron and potassium, figs have been used for their laxative properties for thousands of years. Considered to be one of the most alkaline fruits, they can help to balance a diet high in animal protein and refined foods. The dried fig is a good source of mineral calcium, which can be used in place of dairy foods to help build strong bones.

Grapes and Raisins

Grapes are known to contain major healing properties and are beneficial in treating a variety of ailments from viral infections to herpes outbreaks. Additionally, they are believed to have the ability to flush out the arterial walls of the body. Diuretic and cleansing, grapes are used to rejuvenate the body. Grapes also contain the phytonutrient ellagic acid, which has been shown to prevent the mutation of cancer cells. Grapes are also good for treating arthritis and rheumatism because they contain antioxidant flavonoids.

Raisins are the dried form of grapes and should be soaked in water before using in a smoothie. This soaking helps to reduce the high sugar content, wash off any mold residue, and make them easier to process in a blender.

One cup of grape juice provides 28 milligrams of calcium, 30 milligrams of phosphorus, 0.8 milligrams of iron, 5 milligrams of sodium, 293 milligrams of potassium, and small amounts of vitamins A, B-complex, and C.

Four ounces of raisins provide 34.5 grams of glucose, 34.8 grams of fructose, 1,020 milligrams of potassium, 1 milligram of vitamin C, and 12 milligrams of carotenes.

Mangoes

High in potassium, mangoes are good for helping to regulate high blood pressure and blood circulation. A ripe mango should be firm but have some give when pressed. The skin should be smooth, with a balance of yellow, red, and green coloring. Chinese medicine uses mangoes to help counteract the effects of eating oily foods, because mangoes have the ability to break down fats and animal proteins. In addition, they are good preventatives of cervical cancer because they contain the antioxidant beta-cryptoxanthin. Some people may have an allergic reaction to handling mango skin; however, eating the flesh of the fruit should not cause the same reaction. One mango yields 23 milligrams of calcium, 40 milligrams of phosphorus, 0.9 milligrams of iron, 9 milligrams of sodium, 711 milligrams of potassium, 5,320 IUs of vitamin A, 81 milligrams of vitamin C, and 18 milligrams of magnesium.

Papayas

High in vitamin C and beta-carotene, the papaya has been used traditionally to help with the digestion of proteins. When buying, try to choose a fruit that is soft to the touch and has a deep yellow color. Papaya is at its best when on the verge of being overripe; at this point, the taste and sweetness of the fruit are at their fullest. One medium ripe papaya yields 61 milligrams of calcium, 49 milligrams of phosphorus, 0.9 milligrams of iron, 9 milligrams of sodium, 711 milligrams of potassium, 5,320 IUs of vitamin A, 170 milligrams of vitamin C, and 31 milligrams of magnesium.

Peaches

Peaches are used in traditional Chinese medicine to treat dry conditions of the lungs and inflammation of the stomach. In cases of mild to extreme fever, peach juice can be used for its cooling properties. Because of its water-soluble fiber, the peach can also help to keep cholesterol levels down, thus helping to reduce the risk of heart disease. One ripe peach contains 14 milligrams of calcium, 29 milligrams of phosphorus, 0.8 milligrams of iron, 2 milligrams of sodium, 308 milligrams of potassium, 2,030 IUs of vitamin A, 1.5 milligrams of niacin, 11 milligrams of vitamin C, and 6 milligrams of magnesium.

Pears
The pear tree is one of the earliest cultivated fruit trees, and as a member of the rose family, it is related to the apple. With its high fiber content and the body's slow absorption of its sugar, pears are recommended to keep hunger at bay. They are suitable for people with diabetes, because of their low glycemic index. Traditional Chinese medicine considers the pear to have a cooling effect on the lungs, which helps to eliminate excess mucus and relieve coughs. One ripe pear contains 13 milligrams of calcium, 18 milligrams of phosphorus, 0.5 milligrams of iron, 3 milligrams of sodium, 213 milligrams of potassium, 30 IUs of vitamin A, 7 milligrams of vitamin C, and 9 milligrams of magnesium.

Pineapples
The pineapple is loaded with cancer-preventing phytonutrients. The fruit is often used as a digestive aid because of its large amounts of the enzyme bromelain, which is so powerful it can break down the protein structures in meat. It is best to store an uncut pineapple outside the refrigerator at above 50 degrees. One slice, consisting of a round cut ¼-inch thick, of raw pineapple contains 14 milligrams of calcium, 7 milligrams of phosphorus, 0.4 milligrams of iron, 1 milligram of sodium,

123 milligrams of potassium, 60 IUs of vitamin A, 14 milligrams of vitamin C, and 34 milligrams of magnesium.

Prunes

Renamed "dried plums," prunes have been famous for centuries for their laxative ability. They are an excellent source of iron as they supply 3 milligrams of iron per 8-ounce serving. Prunes are also high in potassium, which helps to regulate blood pressure levels. Soak ²/₃ cup of prunes in filtered water overnight and use both the liquid and fruit in your smoothie. A ²/₃-cup portion of prunes yields 860 milligrams of potassium, 3 milligrams of iron, 38 milligrams of calcium, 155 micrograms of beta-carotene, and 3 micrograms of selenium.

Sweeteners

Refined White Sugar

While refined white sugar may be your sweetener of choice, it is important to understand the role it plays in the function of your endocrine system. In the book *Enzyme Nutrition*, Dr. Edward Howell describes just what happens once sugar enters the body.

> *When (refined) sugar gets into the mouth . . . it throws the endocrine switchboard into helter-skelter. The glands know the organism has been loaded up with a lot of calories but in spite of searching, the nutrients that normally go along with the calories cannot be found in the body. So*

an order to take in more food, in the expectation of getting the important vitamins, minerals, and enzymes, is issued in the form of increased appetite. Eating added sugar in various foods and drinks every day is a way of perpetuating chronic over-stimulation of the pituitary and pancreas glands. The thyroid and adrenals also feel the brunt of the affront. Therefore, far overshadowing the damage resulting from sugar as a carrier of empty calories is its capacity to destroy the delicate endocrine balance and inaugurate a train of pernicious consequences.

All the more reason to eliminate refined sugar and incorporate the natural sweeteners used in the *Simply Smoothies* recipes.

Artificial Sweeteners

Artificial sweeteners, though popular substitutes, are not any better than refined sugar and in some cases can even be worse for you. The popular sweetener aspartame contains phenylalanine, which is absorbed directly into the brain and is extremely toxic to the nervous system. Another very dangerous element of artificial sweeteners is methanol (methyl alcohol, or wood alcohol), which is metabolized into formaldehyde by the body. If you are looking for a sugar substitute, there are plenty of organic alternatives that act as natural sweeteners. The alternatives are known to add nutrients to your diet, as well as provide that wonderful sweet taste.

Natural Sweeteners

Stevia

Stevia is an herb that is 400 times sweeter than sugar but doesn't have the calories or health consequences that sugar does. Known to the Guarani Indians of Paraguay as the "honey leaf," Stevia has been used in the Far East and Europe for the past thirty years to sweeten a multitude of commercial products. Stevia has been prized not only for its sweet qualities but for its ability to aid in digestive disorders, increase glucose tolerance, and help to reduce high blood pressure. Safe for diabetics and those with hypoglycemia, it is known to help regulate blood sugar. Stevia can be used in its raw form, which has a slight licorice aftertaste, or in a processed form that has little or no aftertaste. Stevia comes in powder and liquid ; and can be found in bottles with a small scoop, in individual packets, and as a liquid with a dropper. Because some brands are sweeter than others, each recipe calls for you to add Stevia according to your taste. As a guideline, it is good to remember that $\frac{1}{8}$ teaspoon of Stevia equals 1 teaspoon of sugar or 2 to 4 drops of Stevia liquid. Recipes in this book use a refined white Stevia powder, so adjust the amounts to your taste preference.

Maple Syrup

Made from boiling the sap from the sugar maple tree, it takes 40 gallons of maple sap to make 1 gallon of maple syrup. A concentrated sweetener, it contains the minerals potassium, calcium, manganese, magnesium, phosphorus, and iron. Ounce for ounce, maple syrup has twice as much calcium as milk.

Honey

The "nectar of the gods," honey is in a class by itself when it comes to taste, sweetness, and healing properties. It is best to buy raw, unfiltered honey since many manufacturers dilute honey with water. Honey contains iron, copper, protein, sodium, potassium, and phosphorus. Use it sparingly in your smoothies as it is a very concentrated sweetener.

Honey Water Test

Take a small teaspoon of honey and dip a felt-tipped, water-based ink pen into the honey. If the ink runs, then water has been added.

Fruit Juice Concentrates

Mildly sweet and easy to find in any grocery store, you may want to keep several different varieties of fruit juice concentrate in the freezer to make up the base of your smoothies.

Sucanat

This dehydrated cane juice is rich in minerals and has its own distinctive taste. Use it sparingly, as you would refined white sugar. It is available in most natural food stores.

Fruit Juices

Fruit juices make a great base for your smoothies, and because of their high sugar content, you can opt not to add additional sweetener or cut the amount by half. If you prefer a mild sweetness to your drink, use half juice and half water, or add extra ice cubes. You can find a large selection of organic fruit juices in health food stores and supermarkets. However, most are diluted with grape juice or water. It's best to look for a brand that bottles the pure juice at full strength. Read the labels carefully, as the addition of other ingredients can change the taste of the juice, and not always for the better. For example, coconut milk is oftentimes diluted with white grape juice and a few other ingredients, and the end result does not taste at all like coconut milk. In this instance, it's better to buy a can of unsweetened coconut milk, or make your own, and use this in place of a commercial brand.

Remember, bottled juices have been pasteurized, meaning they have been heated to high temperatures, which kills off many important nutrients in the fruit. Basically, this gives you high sugar without the vitamins

Coconut Milk Recipe

Place 4 cups of warm water in a blender along with 1 cup of grated coconut. Cover and purée for several minutes. Allow to stand for another 10 minutes, then strain and use in your recipes.

to balance it all out. Juicing your own organic fruits and vegetables and then adding them to your smoothie would be the optimal way to obtain the most from your food, though it's not always the quickest or easiest option. Whenever possible, though, try to use fresh fruit juice.

Protein and Meal Powders

Check out the shelves of any health food store and you'll find row upon row of protein powders made from soy, whey, rice, and sprouted grains. Naturally, this can be very confusing for the consumer who is looking for a simple answer. Each powder is a highly concentrated form of protein that is not always easy for the body to digest. While there are schools of thought that recommend the use of protein powders very highly, it is important to educate yourself. Make sure you use a high-quality organic food and take caution not to use it as a daily source of protein. For example, the Ultimate Meal, made by the Ultimate Life company, is a superior meal powder that is not strictly a protein isolate, but a nutrient-dense meal containing a full day's worth of vitamins and minerals.

Nuts and Seeds

Nuts and seeds are loaded with the best kind of protein and fats. Often misunderstood because of their high fat content, nuts and seeds contain iron, zinc, calcium, and potassium, with a number of trace elements. Use as a protein/fat addition in your smoothie or make "nut

Nut Milk

Simply rinse a cup of your favorite nut or seed in water and place in a blender with 3–4 cups of water, then purée for 1–2 minutes. Pour into a jar through a fine mesh strainer or one lined with cheesecloth. At this point, you can add a touch of vanilla extract and some sweetener, cover it, and store it in the refrigerator. The nut milk will keep for up to a week. The best nuts for milking are almonds, coconut, and walnuts, though sunflower, hulled sesame, and pumpkin seeds make a fine beverage as well.

milk" and use as the base for your drink creation. Buy organic when you can, and store them in the refrigerator to keep them fresh longer.

Almonds

Considered to be one of the highest sources of vegetable calcium, almonds are more easily digested when soaked overnight in water or used to make almond milk. Almonds have been considered a valuable addition in the treatment of lung and intestinal difficulties. One cup provides 849 calories, 26.4 grams of protein, 28 grams of carbohydrates, 332 milligrams of calcium, 21.3 IUs vitamin E, 386 milligrams of magnesium, 716 milligrams of phosphorus, 1,098 milligrams of potassium, and 77 grams of fat.

Flax Seeds

Flax seed meal can be a healthful addition to your smoothie creations. Famous for their high fiber content and their effect in lowering cholesterol, flax seeds also contain high amounts of both omega-3 and omega-6 fatty acids. These essential fatty acids (EFAs) are needed as building blocks to form the membranes of billions of cells in the body. The food we eat supplies our daily EFAs. Flax seeds can be ground fresh in a coffee grinder or bought ground and vacuum packed from your local health food store. With the addition of a high-grade flax seed oil taken twice a day, you can be assured of obtaining the essential fats that your body requires.

Sesame Seeds

High in calcium, folate, and iron, sesame seeds are also an excellent source of good fats. One tablespoon of

Sesame Sprinkles

Rinse ½ cup of unhulled sesame seeds in a strainer under running water. Meanwhile, heat a heavy skillet on high until hot, add the drained seeds to the skillet, and stir with a wooden spoon until dry and toasted. Sprinkle some sea salt onto the seeds while toasting. Use the seeds whole or grind them in a mortar and pestle before serving. Store in an airtight container and serve over grains or vegetables. Top a vegetable smoothie with a dash of Sesame Sprinkles.

sesame seeds provides 75 calories, 2.5 grams of protein, 7 grams of fat, 84 milligrams of calcium, 1 milligram of iron, and 13 milligrams of folate.

Peanuts

A member of the legume family, the peanut is a source of both protein and good fat for the body. However, due to the chemicals used in the growing process and the possible presence of aflatoxin, a toxin produced by mold that can grow on peanuts while in storage, it is best to buy organic peanuts and peanut butter to use in your smoothies. One cup of peanuts provides 688 calories, 15 grams of protein, 69 grams of fat, 4 grams of fiber, 4 grams of vitamin E, 94 milligrams of calcium, 3 milligrams of iron, 3 milligrams of zinc, 19 micrograms of selenium, and 66 micrograms of folate.

Walnuts

Delicious when eaten raw or roasted, the walnut is a powerful food known to help prevent heart disease, build a strong immune system, aid the skin in staying hydrated, and supply vitamin B6, which can help alleviate premenstrual symptoms. Walnuts are a good source of omega-3 fatty acids, necessary for blood circulation and brain function.

One cup of raw walnuts provides 651 calories, 14.8 grams of protein, 15.8 grams of carbohydrates, 64 grams of fat, 4 milligrams of vitamin E, 94 milligrams of calcium, 3 milligrams of iron, 3 milligrams of zinc, 19 micrograms of selenium, and 66 micrograms of folate.

Milk and Yogurt

The use of milk and yogurt in blended drinks is popular in many cultures worldwide, documented as far back as ancient India with a drink known as lassi, which is still consumed on a daily basis. Lassi can be either sweet or savory and is a cooling yogurt beverage used to balance the fire in spicy curry dishes. In American culture, milk shakes are commonplace and can be created in any flavor imaginable.

Milk supplies calcium for strong bones, while yogurt settles and strengthens the digestive system. Because there is so much controversy about the high amounts of antibiotics, steroids, and bovine growth hormones used in dairy milk's production, consider using organic whole milks and yogurts or begin to try the diversity of nondairy milks available on supermarket shelves. Milk substitutes are an excellent replacement in smoothies, on cereals, or when baking. Soy, rice, almond, soy/rice, oat, and hazelnut are some of the choices available for you to try, but read the ingredient labels to make sure that they are made with the highest-quality sweeteners and oils. Nondairy milks and soy yogurts also work well for those who have an allergy to animal milk–based products.

Oils

The use of high-quality oils such as flax or hempseed oil increases your intake of omega-3 fatty acids and other important nutrients. One to two tablespoons a day is considered a healthful addition to anyone's diet, and adding them to your smoothie imparts a rich texture and taste. With other seed and nut oils, add the whole nut or seed directly to the recipe in order to obtain all the available nutrients and fiber.

Vegetables

Juicing Fruits and Vegetables

What better way to get your nutrients than from the rich juice of organic fruits and vegetables? The concentration of nutrients in a glass of fresh vegetable juice can contribute to the body's daily requirement of vitamins and minerals. It is a very simple process—you need only a vegetable or fruit juicer and organic produce. It is important to use organic produce because in the process of juicing, you concentrate not only the vegetables and fruits into juice, but also the pesticides that have been sprayed on the produce. This can make for a very toxic cocktail. If organic produce is not available, make sure to scrub your produce well and peel it before juicing.

For those of you interested in getting as much of the valuable fiber as possible from your vegetables, you can experiment with several ways of juicing.

1. Juice half your vegetables first; then place them in a blender with the other half and purée until smooth.
2. Chop your vegetables and add to the blender with enough water to cover them. Start your blender on the lowest setting, then move it to high. Purée until all the ingredients are chopped

and the mixture is smooth. A blended salad is a good example of this process.

3. Juice several different vegetables and add them to the blender with 1 large carrot and purée until smooth.

Vegetable Juice Combinations
1. Carrot, ginger, watercress, celery
2. Celery, kale, carrot
3. Carrot, cucumber, celery
4. Cucumber, carrot, parsley
5. Apple, carrot, ginger
6. Carrot, ginger, coconut milk
7. Grapefruit, orange, lemon
8. Cabbage, carrot, tomato
9. Celery, kale, beet
10. Grape, apple
11. Pineapple, apple, mint
12. Carrot, ginger, beet, lime
13. Beet, carrot, lemon, lime, pineapple
14. Carrot, beet, mango, lime
15. Apple, orange, ginger, mint

The hundreds of varieties of vegetables grown throughout the world make for an impressive list of health-giving nutrients, fiber, and protective phytonutrients. Though not commonly used in smoothie mixtures, there are certain vegetables that lend themselves to the drink and provide a low-calorie, nutrient-rich substitute for a quick meal.

Avocado

The avocado is a fruit commonly known as a vegetable high in fat and calories. Yet the benefits of the avocado far outweigh its health drawbacks. Known for being easy to digest and for its "good" fat and vitamin E content, the avocado is prized for beautifying the skin and lubricating the body's joints. One large avocado provides 190 calories, 20 grams of fat, 8 milligrams of vitamin E, 1,368 milligrams of potassium, and 660 IUs of vitamin A.

Beets

Sweet with a taste of the earth, beets owe their deep red color to betanin, which is also used as a food coloring. Known to stimulate the liver, kidneys, gallbladder, spleen, and bowel, the common beet can also be used to help fight colds. It is a very potent-tasting vegetable; when juicing, use only a quarter of the beet in 8 ounces of mixed vegetable juice. One-third cup of beets yields 380 milligrams of potassium, 8 grams of carbohydrates, 150 micrograms of folate, 1 milligram of iron, 20 micrograms of carotene, 20 milligrams of calcium, and 5 milligrams of vitamin C.

Carrot

Carrots are often used in juice. They contain the highest amount of beta-carotene of any vegetable and are often used to cleanse and purify the blood and organs of the body. Naturally sweet and delicious, they aid in the absorption of iron, while the beta-carotene helps to heal night blindness. One-half cup of carrots provides 5,330 micrograms of carotene, 34 milligrams of calcium, 28 micrograms of folate, 240 milligrams of potassium, 6 grams of carbohydrates, 1 milligram of vitamin E, and 4 milligrams of vitamin C.

Celery

In Chinese medicine, celery is used as a "cooling" food and is considered an excellent blood purifier. Its juice makes a wonderful tonic after the long days of winter and can also be used to treat bladder infections. One large stalk of celery provides 7 calories, 320 milligrams of potassium, 8 milligrams of vitamin C, 41 milligrams of calcium, 50 micrograms of beta-carotene, and 3 milligrams of selenium.

Cucumber

Cucumber is a great skin toner! This humble vegetable has a unique way of cleansing the body and ridding it of old toxins, accumulated waste matter, and chemical residues. Whether juiced or used in a blended salad, cucumber is revered for its youth-promoting action. One cup of raw cucumber yields 26 milligrams of calcium, 260 IUs of vitamin A, 12 milligrams of vitamin C, 13 milligrams of magnesium, 168 milligrams of potassium, and 1.2 milligrams of iron.

Ginger

Chinese medicine considers ginger a warming and stimulating food. It is used to aid digestion and to alleviate motion and morning sickness. A tea made with fresh

Ginger Tea

To prepare 4 cups of ginger tea, peel and chop a 3-inch piece of fresh ginger. Bring 4 cups of pure water to a boil and add the ginger. Reduce the heat and simmer for 10–15 minutes. Allow to sit and cool briefly before serving. Add a teaspoon of raw honey to sweeten.

ginger simmered in water can relieve nausea. Research has found that rheumatoid arthritis and muscular discomfort can also be helped by taking powdered ginger.

Equipment for Making Smoothies

One of the great advantages to making smoothies is that you will need only a few pieces of equipment, the right ingredients, the recipes from this book, and a bit of imagination in order for your meal to come together with speed and ease. Investing in a top-of-the-line blender will give you years of service and the power to efficiently break up ingredients. With so many designs out on the market, which machine will do the work day after day?

Blenders

There are a number of blender styles out there, from high-tech blenders with tons of bells and whistles to the most basic. Depending on your smoothie philosophy, you may find yourself drawn to a certain type of blender. However, the smartest blender choice should follow the "simple is better" rule. A basic bar blender with one switch, a solid metal base, and a stainless steel or glass pitcher with a tight-fitting lid is really the best choice when making smoothies.

If you enjoy the "bells and whistles" approach, you may prefer a blender with a variety of speeds and options for crushing, puréeing, chopping, and grating. When choosing a multifunction blender, however, be sure to select one with a motor strong enough to crush ice, fibrous fruits, and vegetables.

Ice Cubes versus Crushed Ice

The strength of your blender has much to do with whether you should use easily available ice cubes or crushed ice. Ice cubes are more difficult to break apart than crushed ice is, but you will have more control over the quality of the water used in making the ice. Feel free to add or subtract ice to get the thickness that you prefer in your smoothie, or to prevent watering down the taste, freeze juice in ice cube trays and use these in place of ice.

Juicers

For the true smoothie connoisseur, there is nothing like making your own juice from scratch. There are a variety of juicers on the market, and you should know what you are buying before investing $100–$200 on one of them. Here is an overview of what you will find when looking to buy a high-quality juicer.

Centrifugal Force

Most of the electric juicers on the market extract juice by first chopping the fruit or vegetable while spinning at such a high rate of speed that the juice is separated from the pulp. While the pulp remains in the machine, the juice comes out of a spigot into your glass. There is a school of thought that says separating the pulp from the juice can create a blood sugar imbalance in the body, however, and if you're concerned, you can blend the whole food together with water and added ingredients to get the full benefits of the suggested produce.

Mastication

In this particular kind of juicer, the food is ground up and again the pulp is separated from the juice. Although a messier version of the centrifugal force machines, this type of juicer can also be used to make baby foods, nut butters, and ice cream using frozen bananas and other fruit, and can also break down green leafy vegetables.

Juicer/Blender

The Vita-Mix blender is the only machine strong enough to blend vegetables into juice. It can also miraculously make bread, soup, and ice cream just by switching speeds. This machine is a good investment because it performs a number of duties and should last for years.

Other utensils you will need to have on hand for making your smoothies du jour are:

- Measuring cups
- Measuring spoons
- Rubber spatula
- Ice cream scoop
- Ice trays
- Stainless steel strainer

Now that you have the basic understanding of the ingredients you will need, their benefits to your body, and the proper equipment to use to make the process run smoothly, all you need to do is start your blender. Feeding yourself, your family, and your friends with the abundance of creative recipes found in *Simply Smoothies* can open up a whole new taste adventure sure to put some pizzazz into your daily diet routine. Whether you are looking to lose some weight, heal from an illness, have some decadent fun, or just improve your intake of fruits and vegetables, the instructions for making the smoothies in this book will give you all the guidance you will need, plus some useful tips about various foods and their preparation.

Take a moment and look through the contents of your kitchen cupboards and refrigerator. Make a list of the essential smoothie ingredients you would like to have on hand according to your tastes; then head for the grocery store and health food market and pick up the necessities so you can begin right away. Be creative, have fun, and enjoy!

Serving Size

Each recipe featured in this book yields 1 large smoothie or 2 average-size servings.

Chapter 2

Smoothies for Health

In the rush to keep up with the fast pace of daily life, chopping vegetables and cooking a full meal are not often options. How, then, do we provide our bodies with all the nutrients that they need to function? One place to start is with a healthy, delicious smoothie. When you prepare the recipes in this section and substitute them for candy, chips, and pastries, you will notice a gradual increase in your energy and a decrease in your waistline. This is because you will reduce the high amount of fats and refined sugars found in junk foods and replace them with the nutrient-dense ingredients these healthy smoothies call for.

Drinking healthy smoothies in place of a meal or afternoon snack is an excellent way to assist the body in losing unwanted weight. Keep to the ideal of losing two to three pounds a week by consuming plenty of fresh fruits and vegetables, fiber-rich foods, healthy fats, proteins, and carbohydrates while following an exercise routine three to five times per week. The many recipes offered in this chapter contain wholesome ingredients that can satisfy both a sweet tooth and the need for a filling meal.

For children who are picky eaters or who consume soft drinks and high-sugar snack foods, substitute the sweet taste of a healthy smoothie instead. Let them pick the ingredients they would like to have by consulting the Smoothie Ingredients Chart on page 199. This will allow them the opportunity to learn about the many ingredients available for creating sweet and tasty smoothies and to begin to take charge of their own healthy food choices.

Creating a balanced diet using smoothies in place of a meal or snack can also require the addition of certain ingredients that help to supply good fats, fiber, and extra protein. This is where you cross the line into making sure that what goes into the blender will supply your body with essential vitamins and minerals and still continue to taste great. Soy milk, tofu, and soy ice cream can all be substituted for the equivalent in dairy milk, yogurt, and ice cream, giving you a higher yield of protein with less intake of fat and cholesterol. Proteins are the basic building blocks of the human body and are made up of twenty-five different amino acids, fourteen of which the body can manufacture, and eleven that must come from the food we eat. With the intake of adequate amounts of protein, the body is quickly satiated, which helps to prevent overeating. If you are a vegetarian, be particularly careful that you eat enough protein on a daily basis, which can come from beans, legumes, grains, nuts, and soy products.

The importance of EFAs (essential fatty acids) cannot be stressed enough since they are not made by our bodies but must be taken in through diet. For example, linoleic acid, also known as omega-3 fatty acid, can be found in raw nuts and seeds, which provide both protein and high-quality fats that leave the body satisfied when even a small amount is consumed. Flax seed meal is an excellent source of both fiber and omega-3 fatty acids and will aid in weight loss when you take 2–3 tablespoons on a daily basis. Individuals who suffer from constipation will benefit from the way flax meal works to move and cleanse the bowels. Alpha-linolenic acid, or omega-6 acid, is found mostly in fish and helps to keep the blood from clotting. It can also lower the risk of heart disease. All in all, the good news is that the fatty acids are helpful in relieving inflammatory conditions in the body, such as arthritis and psoriasis, while supplying the brain with needed nutrients that can help individuals with attention deficit disorder.

Adding Up the Benefits

Feel free to add any extra ingredients to recipes, such as protein or meal powders, lecithin, flax meal or oil, nuts or seeds.

Pregnant mothers should consume these fatty acids on a daily basis, and children under the age of five years old should be fed omega-3 and -6, along with the highest quality fats. The body needs these fats during times of growth and brain development. It is interesting to note that a human mother's breastmilk is designed to supply the right balance of nutrients to allow for the proper development of the baby's brain. In contrast, cow's milk is geared toward strengthening the young calf's physical body so that he will be able to stand as quickly as possible and move with the herd out of the reach of predators.

When seeking balance in your diet, try to strive for 20 percent fat, 20 percent protein, and 60 percent carbohydrates in the form of fruits, vegetables, and whole grains. Fruits and vegetables should make up the largest part of your carbohydrate intake.

Low-Carb Juice

A quality bottled vegetable juice contains 9 grams of carbohydrates per cup of juice, compared to 27 grams for a cup of apple juice.

This is where "Smoothies for Health" can come in handy with your busy schedule. Each recipe supplies the needed carbohydrates in the form of fruits and vegetables while extra nutrient-dense ingredients can be added depending on your nutrient needs. Try keeping a food journal so you can begin to see just what you are getting and not getting in your diet. Then use these smoothie recipes and our Smoothie Ingredients Chart to guarantee the proper intake of all the essential vitamins and minerals your body needs on a daily basis.

Carrot Orange Smoothie

Serves 1

A very tasty serving of vitamin C and beta-carotene. Try this healthy drink when you're craving that after-dinner snack.

> 1 cup carrot-orange juice
> ½ banana
> 1 tablespoon lecithin
> 1 tablespoon flax meal
> 1 teaspoon flax oil
> 1 scoop rice protein powder
> Stevia to taste
> 4–6 ice cubes (optional)

Combine ingredients in a blender and purée until smooth.

Sugar, Sugar

If you are concerned about consuming too much sugar, then use half juice, half water, and a serving of Stevia. However, you should omit the Stevia powder when using apple juice at full strength, so as not to make the drink too sweet.

Banana Strawberry Protein Smoothie

Serves 1

Now here's a morning meal that will get your day started right with a fantastic blend of fruits, protein, and omega-3 fatty acids.

1 cup water, apple juice, or milk
½ frozen or fresh ripe banana, peeled
4 frozen strawberries
1 tablespoon lecithin granules
1 tablespoon flax seed meal
Stevia to taste
1 scoop non-GMO protein powder
1 teaspoon flaxseed oil

Place ingredients into a blender and purée on high until smooth.

Piña Banana

Serves 1

Missing that hop down to the islands can be remedied with this virgin colada.

1 cup piña colada juice (coconut and pineapple
    combination)
1 frozen banana
6 frozen strawberries

Purée until smooth.

Vegetable Protein Smoothie
Serves 2

Phytonutrients with protein and good fat make this a
health winner. Try this with your favorite sandwich to
give your lunch a lift.

4 carrots
3–4 stalks celery
¼ fresh beet
½ lemon
1 scoop protein powder
1 teaspoon flax seed oil
4–6 ice cubes

1. Wash the vegetables and lemon with a vegetable
   scrub brush and juice in an electric juicer.
2. Transfer the juice to the blender and add the
   protein powder, flax seed oil, and ice cubes.
   Purée briefly—just enough to combine the ingredients—and serve immediately.

All That Jazz

For those of you who like a bit of spice in your life,
you can jazz up vegetable smoothies with the addition of a hot and spicy sauce such as Tabasco
or one of the blue-green algae or spirulina
superfoods.

Bloody Mary Cocktail Smoothie
Serves 1

This tasty concoction may be missing the vodka, but it's not missing out on taste! The perfect way to get your daily dose of veggies.

1 cup mixed vegetable juice
1 teaspoon fresh lemon juice
Few drops hot sauce (to taste)
1 stalk celery
1 cup crushed ice

Purée in a blender until smooth. Serve with celery garnish.

Vegetable Juices

While store-bought veggie juices can be notoriously high in sodium, mixing your vegetable juices at home can be a snap using a vegetable juicer and a blender. If you must buy juice, get a high-quality bottled vegetable juice that contains a combination of juice and fiber. Ingredients can include tomatoes, carrots, celery, spinach, cucumbers, lettuce, beets, watercress, cauliflower, and bell peppers, along with parsley, lime juice, and a hit of jalapeño pepper.

Avocado Veggie Tango

Serves 1

Skeptical about mixing your fruits and veggies? This simple fruit-vegetable combination will not disappoint. So thick and creamy, you can eat it with a spoon!

1 cup mixed vegetable juice
¼ ripe avocado
2 tablespoons plain yogurt
1 teaspoon fresh lemon juice
½ cup crushed ice (optional)

Purée in a blender until smooth.

Brewer's Yeast?

Rich in minerals and trace elements such as selenium, chromium, potassium, magnesium, sodium, copper, manganese, iron, and zinc, and high in eighteen amino acids, brewer's yeast is an excellent protein source for those following a vegetarian diet.

Avocado Protein Smoothie

Serves 1

A true vegetarian delight, this protein-rich meal in a glass is packed with nutrients and good fats to get you through your day.

1 cup mixed vegetable juice
¼ ripe avocado
1 tablespoon brewer's yeast
1 teaspoon fresh lemon juice
1 tablespoon fresh flax seed meal
½ cup crushed ice (optional)

Purée in a blender until smooth. Serve immediately.

Cherry Banana Delight

Serves 1

Exchange the cubes for ⅓ cup cherry juice and ½ cup crushed ice if you forgot to freeze the juice.

1 cup apple juice
3 frozen cubes or ⅓ cup cherry juice
½ cup frozen pitted cherries
½–1 frozen banana

Purée in a blender until smooth.

Soy Vegetable Combination

Serves 1

Protein can come from a surprising variety of sources, which opens up a world of possibilities. Don't be afraid to experiment to get the most out of your smoothies.

> 1 cup fresh carrot juice, juiced with a 2-inch piece
>   of fresh ginger
> 1 teaspoon fresh lemon juice
> 2 tablespoons silken tofu
> Pinch Stevia powder
> ½ cup crushed ice

Purée in a blender until smooth. Serve immediately.

The Tofu Connection

Tofu was originally created in China thousands of years ago to make the soybean more easily digestible by the human body. High in protein and containing essential B vitamins, minerals, calcium, phosphorus, iron, sodium, and potassium, silken tofu is a low-calorie, low-carbohydrate food that works well as a replacement for yogurt in your smoothie recipe.

Tropical Smoothie

Serves 2

An island blend of vitamins, minerals, and natural sweeteners to give your taste buds that extra kick without the extra calories.

1 cup pineapple juice
½ cup unsweetened coconut milk
1 small banana
½ cup pineapple chunks
1 tablespoon honey

Place in the blender and purée on high until smooth.

The Scoop on Ice

For a stronger taste to your smoothie, freeze fruit juice in ice cube trays and add in place of ice cubes or crushed ice.

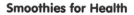

Peaches and Cream

Serves 2

Luscious and velvety, this peach pie flavor is packed with nutrients, not calories. A slice of heaven!

1 cup peach juice
1 cup frozen peaches
½ cup plain yogurt
1 tablespoon raw honey

Purée in a blender, on high, until smooth. Serve immediately.

Banana Ice Cream

Who knew that making banana ice cream could be so simple? Freeze ripe bananas to thicken and sweeten any smoothie creation. Press frozen bananas through a food grinder to make "ice cream." Yum!

Blueberry Soy Shake

Serves 1

This fun, fruity shake is so tasty you'll forget it's packed with goodness! Contains omega-3 fatty acids, proteins, and blueberries, plus the richness of banana for extra texture.

> 1 cup soy-rice milk
> ¼ cup raw walnuts
> ½ cup blueberries
> Stevia to taste
> 1 ripe banana
> 3 ice cubes

Purée in a blender until smooth. Serve immediately.

Orange Banana Cream Dream

Serves 1

Try this refreshing pick-me-up to cool down on a warm day.

> 1 cup organic orange juice
> 2 heaping tablespoons yogurt
> 1 tablespoon honey
> 1 ripe banana

Purée in a blender, on high, until smooth. Serve immediately.

Ginger Grape Eye Opener

Serves 1

This refreshing drink is great to sip on a hot summer night. Great for digestion, with virus-fighting capabilities.

> *1 cup Concord grape juice*
> *1 cup fresh, organic seedless grapes*
> *1-inch piece ginger, peeled*
> *Stevia to taste or 1 tablespoon honey*
> *3 ice cubes*

Purée in a blender, on high, until smooth. Serve immediately.

Grapes That Heal

Revered as a blood tonic, grapes are good for arthritis and rheumatism. In addition, they help to reduce water retention and are recommended for urinary difficulty.

Banana Apple Ginger Smoothie

Serves 1

An apple a day keeps the doctor away. Add a hint of ginger and a banana and you've got a fabulous smoothie.

> *1 cup apple juice*
> *1 ripe banana*
> *½ apple, seeded*
> *1-inch piece ginger, peeled*
> *2 tablespoons maple syrup*
> *3 ice cubes*

Purée in a blender, on high, until smooth. Serve immediately.

Rinse Your Fruit

Raisins, apricots, and prunes should be washed and soaked before using. Rinse in hot water for 1 minute, stirring well; then drain and use in your smoothie. This process helps to clean the dried fruit and make it easier to digest.

Apricots and Orange

Serves 1

The best thing about this light-and-lovely drink isn't the taste—it's that this smoothie is also an antidote for anemia and builds strong blood.

½ cup fresh orange juice
½ cup apricot nectar
½ cup sulfur-free dried apricots,
    soaked in apple juice
Juice of ½ lemon
3 ice cubes

Purée in a blender, on high, until smooth. Serve immediately.

Dried Brown Apricots Are Better

The bright orange apricots have been treated with sulfur dioxide to make them look good. If possible, buy sulfur-free apricots with a rich brown color and you'll find their taste far surpasses the orange ones.

Orange Cream
Serves 1

A vitamin C treat for your inner child and your whole body health.

> *1 cup organic orange juice*
> *2 heaping tablespoons yogurt*
> *1 tablespoon honey*
> *1 cup crushed ice*

Purée in a blender, on high, until smooth. Serve immediately.

Banana Almond
Serves 1

Sit back, relax, and put your feet up. Sip slowly—this recipe is sure to bring a smile.

> *1 cup milk*
> *1 teaspoon almond extract*
> *½ frozen banana*
> *8 frozen strawberries*
> *Stevia to taste*

Purée until smooth.

Raspberry Date Delight

Serves 1

Tart and smooth—a wonderful combination.

> *1 cup pure water*
> *¼ cup frozen raspberry juice concentrate*
> *1 banana*
> *4 pitted dates*
> *3 ice cubes*

Purée in a blender until smooth. Serve immediately.

Raspberries and Seeds

When you use raspberries and blackberries in your smoothies, there will be hundreds of tiny seeds that make the smooth texture of your drink a bit difficult to achieve. These seeds are a vital ingredient of the berry's makeup, however, and are an excellent source of fiber. The best thing to do is to chew slowly and enjoy their many benefits.

Apple Oat Breakfast

Serves 1

Rise and shine, breakfast is ready with the push of a button.

½ cup oat milk
¾ cup apple juice
½ banana
½ teaspoon vanilla
1-inch piece fresh ginger, peeled and chopped
5 frozen strawberries
1–2 teaspoons honey

Purée in a blender until smooth. Serve immediately.

Lucky to Have Oats to Eat

Oats have long been known for their ability to strengthen and rebuild the body when it's weak and deficient. Oat milk is high in silicon and phosphorus for bones and connective tissue, and when ingested on a regular basis, it helps to support the immune system and fight infections.

A Family's Favorite Smoothie
Serves 2–3

Packed with so many great ingredients, this is a smoothie the whole family is sure to love.

1½ cups orange juice
1 ripe banana
1 cup mixed frozen berries
¼ cup plain low-fat yogurt
1 teaspoon vanilla extract
Stevia to taste

Place ingredients in a blender. Blend until smooth. (You may need to add a little spring water to aid blending.)

Healthy Margarita
Serves 1

Tart and sweet, healing, and fun—what more can you ask?

1 cup pomegranate juice
½ cup unsweetened cranberry juice
Stevia to taste
8–10 frozen strawberries

Purée in a blender until smooth. Serve immediately.

Banana Carob Smoothie

Serves 1

This drink is ideal for a midday snack and is also a great treat for allergy sufferers.

1 cup water
¼ cup cashews
1 teaspoon carob powder
½ teaspoon vanilla
1 ripe banana
1 teaspoon honey

Purée in a blender until smooth. Serve immediately.

Mango Lassi

Serves 2

This traditional drink from India is cool, refreshing, and surprisingly simple to make. Serve with your favorite Indian dishes for an authentic meal.

1 cup mango juice
½ cup frozen mango pieces
½ cup yogurt
1–2 tablespoons honey
Fresh mint leaves

Purée in a blender until smooth. Garnish with mint leaves.

Cranberry Apple Delight

Serves 2

The antibacterial benefits of cranberry with the cleansing effects of apple come together in this easy recipe.

> *½ cup unsweetened cranberry juice*
> *1 cup apple juice*
> *½ banana*
> *4 dates*
> *6 frozen strawberries*
> *Stevia to taste or 1 tablespoon honey*

Purée in a blender until smooth.

Apple Yogurt

Serves 1

If you're dying for decadence, try using frozen yogurt instead. Sinfully delicious, without the sin!

> *1 cup apple juice*
> *½ banana*
> *6 frozen strawberries*
> *3 tablespoons vanilla yogurt*

Purée in a blender until smooth.

Apple Orange

Serves 1

This smoothie taste sensation has so many layers of flavor, your tongue is in for a treat.

1 cup apple juice
2 tablespoons orange juice concentrate
½ banana
6 frozen strawberries
3 tablespoons orange yogurt

Purée in a blender until smooth.

Apple Blue

Serves 1

You'll never be blue with this simple and tasty drink. For an extra refreshing touch, garnish with mint leaves.

1 cup apple juice
½ cup blueberry juice
1 cup frozen blueberries

Purée in a blender until smooth.

Apple Blueberry Yogurt

Serves 1

Soft, smooth, and blue. Try frozen yogurt as an alternative to regular yogurt.

1 cup apple juice
½ cup blueberry juice
1 cup frozen blueberries
3 tablespoons blueberry yogurt

Purée in a blender until smooth.

Apple Mango

Serves 2

North meets the tropics in a fine blend of tastes.

½ cup mango juice
1 cup apple juice
1 cup frozen mango pieces

Purée in a blender until smooth.

Apple Mango Lassi
Serves 2

East meets West to soothe a fiery digestive system.

> *1 cup apple juice*
> *½ cup mango juice*
> *½ cup frozen mango pieces*
> *3 tablespoons yogurt*
> *Pinch of cinnamon*

Purée in a blender until smooth.

PomApple
Serves 1

How can something so good be so good for you?

> *1 cup apple juice*
> *½ cup pomegranate juice*
> *6–8 frozen strawberries*
> *½ banana*
> *3 tablespoons vanilla yogurt*

Purée in a blender until smooth. Serve immediately.

Apple Raspberry

Serves 1

When in a hurry, this smoothie is easy to prepare—just remember to chew those seeds.

> *1 cup apple juice*
> *1 cup frozen raspberries*

Purée until smooth. Serve immediately.

Eye Opener

Serves 1

Mid-afternoon slumps can be a thing of the past with this delightful smoothie.

> *1 cup apple juice*
> *¼ cup unsweetened cranberry juice*
> *1-inch piece fresh ginger, peeled*
> *4 frozen strawberries*
> *½ banana*
> *3 tablespoons yogurt*
> *Stevia to taste*

Purée in a blender until smooth.

Chapter 3

Smoothies for Fun

One person's idea of "fun" can differ drastically from another's, especially when it comes to the preparation and taste of food. Throughout most of history, foods that are considered to be fun to eat have traditionally been served during holiday festivities and on special occasions, and have consisted mostly of sugar-laden desserts and ice cream. Now that fun foods have become a part of the everyday diet of most Americans, having something sweet and decadent on occasion can soothe a tired body or ease the burden of a saddened mind. This is acceptable in moderation, but the trouble begins when fun foods replace healthy whole foods as the mainstay of your diet.

Think of your body as a finely tuned machine, much like your car, which needs gas to run, oil to lubricate the parts, and filters that must be changed every so many miles. If you forget to change the oil and filters, your car becomes sluggish and no longer performs as it did when it was new off the lot. Without gas, your car will not run. Likewise, if your joints and tissues are not lubricated with healthful oils and fats, your filtering organs—liver, kidneys, lungs, large intestine, and skin—are not cleansed on a regular basis, and you're not providing fuel in the form of high-quality protein and carbohydrates, your body will not run as well as it should.

From time to time, you can indulge your senses with a decadent dessert if you know that the largest percentage of your food comes from healthy ingredients.

In this chapter, you will find mildly decadent to over-the-top decadent smoothies, depending on the ingredients you choose to use in their preparation. If you're dying for something sweet but reluctant to break your diet, low-fat or nondairy frozen desserts can be substituted for rich high-fat ice cream with little or no change in taste and texture. Carob can be substituted for chocolate, Stevia can replace sugar, and adding more fruit can allow you to eliminate a scoop of ice cream. However, sometimes it's fun to treat yourself and go all out, and this chapter is dedicated to the sweet tooth in all of us!

Pomegranate Slush

Serves 1

Refreshing, sweet, and tart with the deep red color of pomegranate—simply irresistible.

4 ice cubes
1 cup pomegranate juice
1½ tablespoons honey or fructose

Place in a blender and pulse to break up the ice; then purée until smooth. Serve immediately.

Peanut and Banana Smoothie

Serves 1

Peanut butter and banana lovers, you can have their protein and potassium in this rich smoothie while indulging your sweet tooth.

1 cup vanilla rice milk
1 ripe banana
3 tablespoons peanut butter
3 scoops vanilla Rice Dream nondairy frozen
*   dessert*
1 tablespoon honey

Purée in a blender until smooth. Serve immediately.

Pineapple Coconut Slush

Serves 1

A virgin colada that boosts your energy and keeps your head clear.

> *4 ice cubes or 1 cup crushed ice*
> *1 cup pineapple-coconut juice*
> *½ cup pineapple chunks*
> *2 teaspoons honey*

Place ingredients in a blender and pulse to break up the ice; then purée until smooth. Serve immediately.

Raspberry Sorbet Smoothie

Serves 1

Tart and intense with a great finish, this smoothie is the perfect lunchtime refreshment.

> *½ cup pure water*
> *½ cup frozen raspberry juice concentrate*
> *1 cup raspberry sorbet*

Purée in a blender until smooth. Serve immediately.

Classic Milk Shake

Serves 2

Still decadent, still delicious, and always a crowd pleaser!
Add your favorite syrups or fruit to this recipe and have
a blast.

1½ cups milk
1 cup vanilla ice cream
½ teaspoon vanilla extract

Purée in a blender until smooth. Serve immediately.

Ice Cream, You Scream

When it comes to ice cream, you know best what
you like, so feel free to substitute your favorite flavor
of ice cream in this classic recipe. Choose a brand
with swirls of chocolate, fruit, cookies, or chips to go
with your smoothie. Feel free to change and adapt
this recipe to suit your tastes and needs—after all,
it's your smoothie.

Carob Hazelnut Treat

Serves 1

A fabulous dessert drink no matter how you look at it—hazelnuts and carob milk combine for a sweet and calming flavor that's sure to impress.

1 cup carob rice milk
½ banana
1 teaspoon hazelnut extract
3 tablespoons yogurt
Stevia to taste

Purée in a blender until smooth.

The Carob Pod

Carob is often used as a replacement for chocolate in drinks and candies. It is naturally sweet and rich in calcium and minerals. To make your own carob milk, you will need to purchase carob powder from the health food store. Using your choice of milk, add 1 heaping tablespoon of carob powder and stir to blend well.

PJ-OJ
Serves 2

A vitamin C tropical milk shake to satisfy that sweet tooth and provide a vitamin boost.

> *1 cup pineapple juice*
> *1 tablespoon frozen orange juice concentrate*
> *½ cup milk*
> *1 tablespoon honey*
> *½ cup crushed ice or 3 ice cubes*

Purée in a blender until smooth. Serve immediately.

Apple Tart Smoothie
Serves 1

Immune support at any time you need a lift.

> *1 cup carrot-orange juice*
> *Juice of 1 lemon*
> *2 tablespoons raw honey*
> *1 small apple, cored and chopped*
> *½ tablespoon fresh ginger, chopped*
> *2–3 ice cubes or ½ cup crushed ice*

Purée in a blender until smooth. Serve immediately.

Carob and Vanilla Milk Smoothie

Serves 1

Get your daily dose of potassium in a fun shake. For an extra kick, add a couple of strawberries or blueberries into the mix.

1 cup carob rice or soy milk
1 teaspoon vanilla
2 heaping scoops vanilla ice cream
½ large banana

Purée in a blender until smooth. Serve immediately.

Banana Scoop

Bananas help to detoxify the body and can help intestinal troubles such as diarrhea, colitis, and hemorrhoids. An excellent source of potassium, bananas, along with a whole-foods diet, can also aid in lowering blood pressure.

Carob Chip Smoothie

Serves 1

Is this smoothie healthy? Better than most and still delicious!

1 cup carob milk
1 teaspoon vanilla
1 cup carob ice cream
3 tablespoons carob chips
½ large banana

Purée in a blender until smooth. Serve immediately.

Chocolate-Covered Strawberries

Serves 1

Let's just say this is a smoothie "to die for"!

1 cup chocolate milk
3 scoops chocolate ice cream
8 frozen strawberries
1 teaspoon vanilla

Purée in a blender until smooth. Eat with a spoon.

Nutty Carob Vanilla Milk Shake

Serves 1

Get your milk shake fix with a great mix of protein, carbs, and good fat.

1 cup milk
1 teaspoon vanilla
3 heaping scoops vanilla ice cream
½ large banana
¼ cup walnuts
6 dates

Purée in a blender until smooth. Serve immediately.

Peanut Butter and Jelly

Serves 2

We grew up eating this on white bread—here's a fun new twist! Substitute your favorite fruit and fruit jelly in place of cherries for a little variety.

½ cup unsweetened coconut milk
1 cup milk
1 heaping tablespoon peanut butter
½ cup frozen cherries
½ banana
1–2 tablespoons cherry jelly

Purée in a blender until smooth. Serve immediately.

Chocolate Coconut Decadence
Serves 2

I have to confess, this smoothie is all about the calories!
But it's worth the indulgence.

> *1 cup chocolate milk*
> *½ cup unsweetened coconut milk*
> *3 scoops chocolate ice cream*
> *⅓ cup chocolate chips*
> *½ teaspoon almond extract or*
> *1 tablespoon roasted almond butter*

> Purée in a blender until smooth.

Blackberry Ice Delight
Serves 1

Fresh, in-season blackberries are best, but frozen organic
ones will work great as well. Enjoy the tastes of summer
with this refreshing drink.

> *1 cup apple juice*
> *½ cup ripe blackberries*
> *1 cup vanilla ice cream*

> Purée in a blender until smooth. Serve immediately.

Black Forest Smoothie
Serves 1

You will think you died and woke up in heaven when you sip this chocolaty, fruity drink.

1 cup chocolate milk
3 scoops chocolate ice cream
⅓ cup unsweetened ground coconut
½ cup frozen cherries

Purée in a blender until smooth. Eat with a spoon.

Crunchy Smoothie

If you like some crunch with your smoothies, add the chips, coconut, nuts, or frozen fruit at the end of blending and pulse the switch to create a chunky rather than smooth texture to your smoothie.

Blackberry Sorbet Low-Fat Delight

Serves 1

Who says low fat can't be delicious? This tasty concoction is the perfect pick-me-up.

1 cup apple juice　　　　*½ cup ripe blackberries*
1 cup blackberry sorbet

Purée in a blender until smooth. Serve immediately.

Rocky Road

Serves 1

Nuts, chocolate, and ice cream make for a traditional combination of tastes and textures in this recipe. Leave the chunks large or blend them right into the liquid—let your taste buds be your guide.

1 cup milk
1 cup vanilla ice cream
¼ cup chocolate syrup
2 tablespoons dark chocolate chips
2 tablespoons walnuts, chopped

1. Purée milk, ice cream, and syrup in a blender until smooth.
2. Add the chips and walnuts and pulse to blend. Serve immediately.

Apple Pie à la Mode

Serves 2

Using applesauce gives this smoothie a creamy consistency with the richness of apples and the spices of an oven-baked pie.

> 1 cup apple juice
> ½ cup applesauce
> 3 scoops vanilla ice
>   cream
> ¼ teaspoon nutmeg
>
> ½ teaspoon cinnamon
> ¼ teaspoon ginger
>   powder

Purée in a blender until smooth. Serve immediately.

Carob Strawberry Wonder

Serves 1

Carob can stand on its own when it comes to taste, and when you add the benefits of its energizing properties, the vitamin C from the strawberries, and the cleansing property of cardamom, this rich shake can be enjoyed without guilt.

> 1 cup frozen strawberries
> 1 cup carob Rice Dream
> ½ cup carob milk
> ½ teaspoon cardamom powder

Purée until smooth. Serve immediately.

Canta-Loopy

Serves 2

If you are loopy for cantaloupe and ice cream, then here is a combination that will truly thrill your taste buds.

> *1 cup milk*
> *1 cup ripe cantaloupe pieces*
> *3 scoops vanilla ice cream*
> *½ teaspoon grated fresh ginger*

1. Place the first three ingredients in the blender; then grate the ginger on the fine setting of a vegetable grater.
2. To extract the juice, squeeze the pulp of the ginger into the blender and purée until smooth. Serve immediately.

Cherry Chocolate Jubilee

Serves 1

Try using cherry vanilla ice cream for a double dip of cherries. The extra sweetener can be omitted if it is too sweet for your taste buds.

> *1 cup frozen cherries*
> *3 tablespoons dark chocolate chips*
> *1 tablespoon sweetener*
> *¼ cup kirsch*
> *3 scoops vanilla ice cream*

Purée until smooth. Serve immediately.

Chocolate Raspberry

Serves 1

You should use the darkest chocolate ice cream possible for this one, and if you want to send it over the top, make sure it has a vein of rich fudge.

> *1 cup double chocolate ice cream*
> *½ cup frozen raspberries*
> *¼ cup framboise liqueur*
> *1 cup vanilla rice milk*

Purée in a blender until smooth. Serve immediately.

Banana Foster

Serves 1

This fun smoothie can be made without the rum and still retain its decadent status. Replace the liquor with ¼ teaspoon of rum extract to receive the full taste effect.

> *1 ripe banana*
> *1 tablespoon maple syrup*
> *1 ounce rum*
> *1 cup vanilla ice cream*
> *½ cup milk*

Purée in a blender until smooth. Serve immediately.

Pumpkin Pie

Serves 1

This nondairy smoothie is just as delicious as the version using heavy cream.

> *1 cup vanilla rice milk*
> *½ cup canned cooked pumpkin purée*
> *2 tablespoons maple syrup*
> *1 teaspoon vanilla extract*
> *¼ teaspoon cinnamon*
> *¼ teaspoon allspice*
> *3 scoops vanilla Rice Dream frozen dessert*

Purée in a blender until smooth. Serve immediately.

Orange Chocolate Rum Cake

Serves 1

If you've ever dipped orange slices into chocolate, then you know the outstanding effect this taste combination can have. If you decide to omit the rum, add ¼ teaspoon of rum extract instead.

1 cup fresh orange juice
1 cup double chocolate ice cream
Zest of ½ orange
1 ounce dark rum
½ teaspoon vanilla extract
2 honey graham crackers, broken into pieces

1. Purée the first five ingredients in the blender until smooth.
2. Add the graham crackers and pulse a few times just to blend. Serve immediately.

Key Lime Pie

Serves 1

Here is the unofficial smoothie version of a Florida Key lime pie, which is best enjoyed while watching the sun set at the beach.

> 1 cup lime sherbet
> Juice of 1 lime
> ¼ cup unsweetened coconut milk
> ¼ cup milk
> 1–2 tablespoons honey
> 1 ounce tequila (optional)

Purée in a blender until smooth.

Lemon Meringue

Serves 1

Lemon lovers, get ready to pucker up and indulge with this version of the classic American pie recipe.

> Zest of ½ lemon   ⅓ cup milk
> Juice of 1 lemon   Stevia to taste
> 1 cup lemon sorbet
> ½ cup vanilla ice cream

Purée in a blender until smooth. Top with whipped cream and serve immediately.

Crunchy Peach Pie

Serves 1

When peaches are ripe and in season, you can use them freshly skinned and pitted in this recipe; then slice some extras and freeze them in preparation for the next batch.

1 cup milk
½ cup fresh or frozen
    peach slices
½ teaspoon vanilla

Juice of ½ lemon
3 scoops peach ice cream
1–2 tablespoons honey
6 vanilla wafers, broken

1. Purée the first six ingredients in a blender until smooth.
2. Add the wafers and pulse to blend.

Carob–Almond Butter Smoothie

Serves 1

Carob is an excellent replacement for chocolate, with a natural sweetness and a distinctive taste all its own. Paired with almond butter, it's a winner.

1 cup rice milk
3 tablespoons almond butter
1 tablespoon carob powder

½ teaspoon vanilla
Stevia to taste
½ cup crushed ice

Purée in a blender until smooth. Serve immediately.

Charlotte Russe

Serves 1

This version is perfect for those of you who like a smooth and creamy texture with a cookie crunch surprise and the sweetness of jam.

> 1 cup milk
> ½ teaspoon vanilla
> 1 cup vanilla ice cream
> 1 ounce raspberry liqueur or brandy (optional)
> 2 tablespoons raspberry jam
> 6 vanilla wafers, broken into pieces

1. Purée the first four ingredients in the blender until smooth.
2. Add the jam and wafers and pulse a few times to blend. Serve immediately.

Spice and Fruit Cream

Serves 1

Keeping some of the dried fruit in chunks allows for a satisfying chew while enjoying this recipe. For a softer texture, soak the raisins while you gather the rest of the ingredients.

1 cup milk
1 cup vanilla ice cream
¼ teaspoon cinnamon
Pinch nutmeg
Pinch ground cloves
¼ teaspoon powdered
  ginger
½ teaspoon vanilla
3 tablespoons raisins
4 pitted dates

Purée in a blender, leaving some of the fruit in chunks for chewing. Serve immediately.

Mulled Cider Smoothie

Serves 1

Whether sitting in front of a roaring fire on a winter's night or celebrating the Fourth of July, this indulgent smoothie allows you to have your daily apple and eat it, too.

1 cup apple juice
1 apple, peeled and cored
3 tablespoons raisins, soaked
Pinch ground cloves
¼ teaspoon cinnamon
Pinch nutmeg
3 scoops vanilla ice cream

Purée in a blender until smooth. Serve immediately.

Pineapple Upside-Down Cake

Serves 1

A classic American recipe that was the standard in many households, here it's a smoothie turned upside down in the blender and topped with wafer crumbs.

1 cup pineapple juice
½ cup fresh pineapple
1 tablespoon maple syrup
3 scoops vanilla ice cream
6 vanilla wafers, crushed

1. Purée the first four ingredients in the blender until smooth.
2. Pour into a wide-mouthed glass and sprinkle the wafers on top. Serve immediately.

Cookies and Cream

Serves 1

You can always use cookies-and-cream ice cream in this version, but then you won't get to control just how many of those chocolate and cream temptations you can add.

1 cup milk
1 cup vanilla
    ice cream

6 chocolate wafers with
    vanilla cream, broken
    into pieces

1. Purée the first two ingredients in the blender until smooth.
2. Add the cookie pieces and pulse to blend according to your size preference.

Coconut Macaroon

Serves 1

If all you are using is sweetened coconut and milk, just be sure to omit the honey or adapt it to your taste.

⅔ cup milk
¼ cup unsweetened coconut milk
2 tablespoons unsweetened coconut
½ teaspoon vanilla
2 tablespoons honey
1 cup vanilla ice cream

Purée in a blender until smooth. Serve immediately.

Coconut Pecan Smoothie

Serves 1

For those of you who love the taste of coconut ice cream, you know how hard it is to find in grocery stores. Fear not—with this recipe your searching is over. For a more intense coconut taste, increase the amount of coconut milk and adjust by adding extra frozen yogurt.

1 cup vanilla frozen yogurt
½ teaspoon vanilla
2–3 tablespoons honey
¼ cup unsweetened coconut milk
2 tablespoons unsweetened dried coconut
3 tablespoons roasted pecans, chopped

1. Purée the first four ingredients in the blender until smooth.
2. Add the coconut and pecans and pulse to blend.

Orange Cranberry Torte

Serves 2

The frozen yogurt and juice help to give a bit of tartness to this recipe, as well as a whopping dose of vitamin C. Sprinkle the walnuts on top for a grand finale.

1 cup orange frozen yogurt
1 cup fresh orange juice
¼ cup unsweetened cranberry juice
4–6 pitted dates
Stevia to taste
1 tablespoon walnuts, chopped

1. Purée the first five ingredients in the blender until smooth.
2. Pour into a glass and top with the walnuts. Serve immediately.

Banana Split

Serves 1

Remember the first time you ate a banana split and you were amazed that all of that was for you? Well, here it is again, rich, cool, and full of all the same delicious ingredients—and it's all for you.

1 cup milk
1 scoop vanilla ice cream
1 scoop cherry ice cream
1 scoop strawberry ice cream
½ cup fresh or frozen cherries
1 ripe banana
2 tablespoons chocolate sauce
Whipped cream

1. Purée the first four ingredients in a blender until smooth.
2. Add more milk to thin, less milk to thicken.
3. Add the cherries and banana and pulse to break into small pieces.
4. Pour into a tall glass and drizzle with chocolate sauce. Top with whipped cream and a cherry.

Nutty Turtle

Serves 1

There's the chocolate-covered candy and then there's the smoothie version. When comparing one to the other, you will see that there is just no comparison.

1 cup milk
3 scoops pralines and cream ice cream
3 tablespoons pecans, chopped
1 tablespoon caramel topping
1 tablespoon chocolate sauce
Whipped cream

1. Purée the milk and ice cream in a blender until smooth.
2. Add the pecans and pulse to blend. Pour into a tall glass and drizzle with the caramel and chocolate. Top with whipped cream.

Chapter 4

Exotic Fruit Smoothies

What makes a drink exotic and mysterious is all in the ingredients used and how they are put together. When experienced away from their place of origin, fruits from other countries can be a strange and exciting taste adventure with promises of exotic smells and taste sensations. In supermarkets, green grocers, and Asian markets across the country, a wide variety of tropical fruits are available to everyone at affordable prices. Because of the tremendous diversity of cultures living in both urban and rural areas of America, you can now find ripe mangoes alongside papaya, pineapple, and kiwi fruit. In the freezer section of many large food stores, bags of frozen exotic fruits keep company with strawberries, blueberries, and melon, all peeled, sliced, and waiting to be make into the perfect smoothie.

Although the words *exotic, unusual,* and *imported* may give these fruits a certain allure, rest assured that they are revered in their native countries for their high nutrient value and health benefits. It is important to buy these fruits fresh and unbruised, making sure to use them when ripe and soft to the touch. With ripe papaya, a touch of lemon always gives a zip of flavor, whether you use the whole fruit or just the juice. Keep in mind that the mango is a very sweet fruit when ripe, so adjust the use of sweetener in your smoothie to account for your particular taste preference. To tell if a pineapple is ripe, pluck a leaf from its top. If it pulls away without a fight, you have a pineapple ready to be eaten.

Open your mind and taste buds and trust your wild self when putting together these exotic smoothie recipes in this chapter. Think of it as taking a tropical vacation without leaving your kitchen!

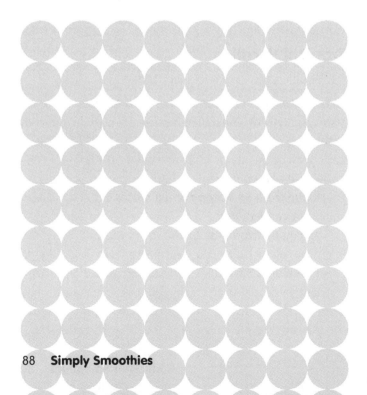

Moroccan Surprise

Serves 1

This combination of cool fruits and smooth flavors is sure to satisfy your thirst.

½ cup pineapple juice
½ cup pomegranate juice
1 tablespoon raw unfiltered honey
½ cup frozen peaches
2–3 ice cubes

Purée in a blender until smooth. Serve immediately.

Tropical Vacation

Serves 1

A fantastic way to taste a bit of the tropics, mon. No plane tickets or sunscreen necessary—just bring your taste buds.

1 cup mango juice
1 cup fresh or frozen mango pieces
½ frozen banana
Juice of 1 fresh lime

Purée until smooth.

Tropical Date Smoothie

Serves 2

Packed with vital nutrients and tons of taste, this fabulous concoction really hits the jackpot.

½ cup pineapple juice
½ cup papaya juice
⅓ cup unsweetened coconut milk
½ large banana
6 pitted dates
Stevia to taste or 1 tablespoon honey

Purée in a blender until smooth. Serve immediately.

Tropical Fruit

To ensure that you have the right fruit on hand for these recipes, buy mangoes, papaya, and even pineapples when ripe and in season. Peel, seed or core, and cube them; then freeze in airtight containers or freezer bags.

Sunshine Smoothie
Serves 1

This fun and simple recipe is sure to brighten your day, no matter what the weather may bring!

1 cup papaya juice
½ large banana
1 tablespoon raw honey
1 tablespoon frozen orange juice concentrate
2 ice cubes

Purée in a blender until smooth.

Codependent Papaya Smoothie
Serves 1

This drink is great for digesting the good fats while assimilating vitamins and minerals. But don't let all of that scientific stuff fool you—it's also fun to drink.

1 cup papaya juice
¼ cup unsweetened coconut milk
1 teaspoon raw honey
½ large banana
3 ice cubes

Purée in a blender until smooth.

Exotic Stimulation
Serves 1

The crisp tang of ginger and sweet smooth papaya make this drink cleansing and stimulating at the same time.

> ⅔ cup pineapple juice
> ½ cup papaya
> 1½-inch piece fresh ginger, peeled and chopped
> ½ large banana
> 3 tablespoons vanilla yogurt
> 1 tablespoon honey or Stevia to taste

Purée in a blender until smooth.

Cranberry Pineapple Cleanser
Serves 2

Packed with flavor and vital nutrients, this recipe is chock-full of bacteria fighters and blood cleansers sure to keep you healthy and wise.

> ⅓ cup unsweetened cranberry juice
> ½ cup water
> ½ cup pineapple juice
> 3 tablespoons vanilla yogurt
> ½ large banana
> 1 tablespoon honey or Stevia to taste

Purée in a blender until smooth.

CranPapaya Smoothie

Serves 2

This enzyme-rich smoothie is a rich and healthy palate pleaser.

> ½ cup unsweetened cranberry juice
> ½ cup water
> ½ cup papaya juice
> 3 tablespoons vanilla yogurt
> ½ large banana
> 1 tablespoon honey or Stevia to taste

Purée in a blender until smooth.

PopPomp Smoothie

Serves 1

Papayas, pomegranates . . . perfect! This fun summer drink is smooth, tart, and stimulating.

> ¾ cup papaya juice
> ¼ cup pomegranate juice
> 1-inch piece fresh ginger, peeled and chopped
> ½ large banana
> 2 tablespoons yogurt
> 1 tablespoon protein powder
> 1 tablespoon honey or Stevia to taste

Purée in a blender until smooth.

Melon Deluxe Duo

Serves 1

Melons are one of the tastiest treats of summer, and they make for fabulous smoothies. For a little extra creaminess, add plain or vanilla yogurt to taste.

¼ large, cold honeydew melon, peeled and seeded
¼ large, cold cantaloupe, peeled and seeded

Place cubed melon in a blender and purée until smooth. Serve immediately.

Melon Surprise

What a surprise it is to see how melon froths into the perfect smoothie without any help but the whir of a blender. This is nature's recipe for a mono-fruit smoothie. Try using honeydew melon or cantaloupe solo to experience the depth of its flavor. Most important, keep the melon cold before adding it to the blender.

Virgin Margarita

Serves 1

A no-fail way to get the party started, with or without the tequila. The extreme sweetness of Stevia combines well with the sour of limes here.

> *Juice of 2 limes*
> *1 cup water*
> *Stevia to taste*
> *1 cup crushed ice*

Purée until smooth.

Enzyme Papaya

Serves 1

This tart and tasty drink is great for your digestion, and even better for your skin.

> *1 cup papaya juice*
> *1 cup frozen papaya pieces*
> *Juice of ½ lime*

Purée until smooth.

Good Guava!

Serves 1

Bring the islands to your kitchen with this combination of tropical fruits. If using fresh instead of frozen fruit, add ½ cup chopped ice.

1 cup guava juice
½ cup frozen papaya pieces
½ cup frozen mango pieces
Juice of 1 lime

Purée until smooth.

Tropical Heaven

Serves 2

This healthy, heavenly drink is the perfect refreshment to enjoy with friends.

1 cup papaya juice
½ cup pineapple juice
½ cup frozen mango pieces
½ cup frozen papaya pieces
½ banana
Juice of 1 lime

Purée until smooth.

MangApple Combo

Serves 1

Try this simple smoothie for a sweet, tart lift to the spirit after a long day of work.

½ cup mango juice
½ cup apple juice
1 small sweet apple, cored
Juice of ½ lemon
1 tablespoon raw honey
½ cup crushed ice

Purée until smooth.

Apple Pear Bear

Serves 1

"Chew your drink, and drink your food," so the saying goes.

1 cup apple juice
½ fresh apple, cored
½ fresh pear, cored
½ teaspoon cinnamon
1 tablespoon honey
1 cup crushed ice

Purée until smooth.

Apple Blue Moon

Serves 1

This easy recipe is sure to be a hit! Phytochemicals for the brain, sweetness for your soul.

1 cup apple juice
1 cup frozen blueberries
3 tablespoons vanilla yogurt

Purée until smooth.

Mango Colada

Serves 2

Ripe mangoes freeze beautifully and are a wonderful smoothie ingredient. Be sure to purchase a ripe mango. Peel, seed, cube, and then freeze. So simple, so delicious!

1 cup piña colada juice (pineapple and coconut
*   combination)*
½ cup mango juice
½ frozen banana
½ cup frozen mango pieces

Purée until smooth.

Virgin Colada

Serves 1

A nonalcoholic take on the traditional tropical favorite. The best news is that this recipe happens to be good for you.

> *1 cup piña colada juice (pineapple and coconut combination)*
> *2 tablespoons shredded coconut*
> *1 cup frozen pineapple pieces*
> *½ cup crushed ice*

Purée until smooth.

Sweet Coconut

Most commercial coconut has been oversweetened with refined sugar. It's best to use unsweetened, grated coconut. Or, to make your own, buy a fresh coconut and wrap it in a kitchen towel. Hit it with a hammer to crack the shell. Drain the water into a measuring cup and taste for sweetness. If it has a musty taste, it has gone rancid and should be discarded. If the water tastes fresh and sweet, you can use it in your smoothie. Take a dull knife and slide it between the shell and the meat, prying the meat out of the shell. With a sharp knife or vegetable peeler, peel the brown skin away from the white meat. Cut the meat into large pieces and grate on the large holes of a box grater. This should yield almost 3 cups of grated coconut, which you can add to your smoothies or use to make coconut milk.

Strawberry Colada

Serves 1

Think spring with this light, festive drink. Coconut and strawberries are the perfect combination for this frothy treat.

> *1 cup piña colada juice (pineapple and coconut*
> *combination)*
> *¼ cup unsweetened coconut milk*
> *8 frozen strawberries*
> *Stevia to taste*
> *1 cup crushed ice*

Purée until smooth.

Fruit Veggie Combo

Serves 1

What better way than a delicious, nutritious smoothie to get your daily intake of fruits and veggies? Buy packaged fruit/veggie juice for easy convenience.

> *1 cup Vruit (fruit/vegetable juice)*
> *½ frozen banana*
> *6 frozen strawberries*

Purée until smooth.

Chapter 5

Healing Smoothies

*"Let food be your medicine and
medicine your food."*—Hippocrates

Living on the Greek island of Kos during the fifth century B.C., Hippocrates, the father of modern medicine, used food to treat and heal his patients. Much of what he taught so long ago—that the human body needs the right balance of foods, proper exercise, and fresh air and water to ensure optimal health and well-being—is recognized today by the medical profession as good advice. In ancient times, all medications came from plants, and even today there are pharmaceutical drugs that are still derived from nature.

In the past twenty years, the allopathic medicine establishment has begun to show an interest in a more holistic approach to healing the body. A holistic approach views the human body as a whole system that integrates the physical body, mind, and spirit; the modern medical approach, on the other hand, sees it as separate parts and pieces. When treating the body as a whole, the holistic approach seeks to heal the cause of disease rather than merely treat the symptoms. In India, China, and Japan, there are integrated forms of treating illness with food and herbs that are influencing our Western methods of treatment, each of them based on the simple premise of achieving balance within our physical ecosystem.

Our ancestors brought with them to America the healing knowledge of herbs and foods that they had learned from their families and village doctors. Once here, through experimentation, practice, and patience they had to find native plants that could duplicate what they had left behind. Ironically, many of the plants once considered to be of great medicinal value are now viewed as mere weeds and sprayed with poisons each season to ensure their demise. Plant-based medicines may take longer to heal the body, but they cause few or no side effects and less disruption to the body's natural ecology.

Simple herbal teas, organically grown and brewed for medicinal purposes, can be a powerful antidote for common ailments such as a cold, fever, indigestion, headache, liver stagnation, and bladder infections. Fruit and vegetable juices aid in the healing of a number of diseases and chronic problems, while a balance of the proper foods high in nutritional value helps to support and build a strong immune system. When a person is ill, his or her appetite can become suppressed or the digestive system may be too weak to handle solid foods. At other times, inflammation in the body can cause pain and weakness, and a stagnant liver can slow down the whole system and begin to poison the bloodstream with toxins. Blending juices, along with the whole fruit or vegetable can be a way to provide nutritious meals during these weak times. This is where the Healing Smoothies recipes can be used to help supply the necessary nutrients without putting stress on the digestive system and providing nutritious intake of foods for those too weak to chew their food completely.

Our blood is the river of life that runs through every part of our body, carrying nutrients to every cell, organ, and tissue. However, it also receives toxic debris filtered through our liver, kidneys, lungs, and intestines, which can eventually poison the body's fragile ecosystem if left to build up. Eating a whole-foods diet, which consists of the highest quality foods such as fruits, vegetables, whole grains, beans, legumes, nuts, seeds, and moderate amounts of animal protein and dairy, can keep the "river" clean of those poisons and help to prevent disease from taking root in the body. Supplementing a meal or snack with a healthy smoothie is a great way to stay healthy, but if illness does occur, there are natural alternatives to taking a pill that can be found in a combination of foods and juices that have been used throughout the ages to heal and cleanse the body of illness and disease. Enjoy these recipes for Healing Smoothies to help fight or prevent illness, or as a healthful snack to keep you going throughout the day.

Cranberry Cocktail

Serves 1

Cranberry juice is well known for the treatment of bladder infections. Here is an excellent smoothie using cranberry juice and vitamin C to acidify the urine. It also happens to taste great.

> *1 cup orange juice*
> *⅓ cup unsweetened cranberry juice*
> *8 frozen strawberries*
> *Stevia to taste or 1 tablespoon honey*

Purée in a blender until smooth. Serve immediately.

Not Just for Sauce

Cranberry juice is recommended for bladder infections as it prevents the bacteria from adhering to the walls of the bladder. Vitamin C helps to acidify the urine and fight the infection.

Cranberry Vitamin C Smoothie

Serves 1

Tart, sweet, and loaded with bacteria fighters. Whip up this healthful drink just before cold season hits, to ward off infection.

> ½ cup unsweetened cranberry juice
> 1 cup water
> Stevia to taste
> 1 gram vitamin C powder
> ½ cup crushed ice

Purée in a blender until smooth. Serve immediately.

Ginger Lemon Cough Remedy

Serves 1

This will help cool the fever of a summer cold.

> Juice of 2 lemons
> 1 cup water
> 2 tablespoons raw honey
> 1½-inch piece fresh ginger, peeled and grated
> ½ cup crushed ice (optional)

1. In a blender, combine the lemon juice, water, and honey.
2. Squeeze the grated ginger into the mixture, add the ice, and purée until smooth. Serve immediately.

Antibiotic Cold Fighter

Serves 1

Garlic is a natural antibiotic, and with the help of immune-boosting vegetable juice, you can continue to fight off the bad guys.

½ cup carrot juice
¼ cup celery juice
¼ cup beet juice
1 medium carrot, scrubbed and chopped
Juice of ½ lemon
1 clove garlic

Purée in a blender until smooth.

The Miracle of Garlic

Garlic has long been known for its antibacterial, antiviral, and antifungal properties. It supports and strengthens the immune system, helps to lower cholesterol, and is used to complement conventional anticancer therapies.

Lemon–Garlic Syrup Wonder Drink

Serves 1

A powerful remedy for many ailments from sore throats to seasonal colds—or even as a preventive in the pre-cold season.

>   *1 cup filtered water*
>   *1 tablespoon garlic syrup (Recipe follows)*
>   *Juice of 1 lemon*
>   *Stevia to taste*
>   *6 ice cubes*

Purée in a blender until smooth. Serve immediately.

Garlic Syrup

Peel and press 1 head of garlic into a jar. Add ½ cup of raw, unfiltered apple cider vinegar and ½ cup distilled water. Cover and shake the jar. Let stand for 4 hours. Strain and add ¼ cup of vegetable glycerin or honey, mix well, and keep refrigerated. Take 1 tablespoon 3 times a day for nearly all purposes, but be sure to dilute it with 1 cup of water. Do not take undiluted.

A Blended Salad

Serves 1

When it is difficult to chew solid food and you need nutrients, prepare this smoothie as a meal and eat slowly. This smoothie is packed with vitamins and nutrients!

1 cup filtered water
¼ ripe avocado
1 handful fresh spinach (washed)
Juice of 1 lemon
1 clove garlic
2 tablespoons Bragg's Liquid Aminos
¼ cup silken tofu
3 ice cubes

Purée in a blender until smooth. Serve immediately.

Blended Salad

Omit the ice cubes and use this as a creamy salad dressing on a bed of greens with baked tofu and toasted almonds.

Blended Salad II

Serves 1

Experimentation is key to creating your own special smoothies. Here's another great variation for you to try.

1 cup mixed vegetable juice
¼ ripe avocado
1 handful mesclun greens
2 tablespoons raw apple cider vinegar
¼ cup soft cooked brown rice
2 tablespoons Bragg's Liquid Aminos
1 garlic clove

Blend until smooth. Serve immediately.

Apple Lemon Garlic Tonic

Serves 1

Fresh apple juice provides extra nutrients and taste to the healing powers of garlic.

1 cup fresh apple juice
½ raw apple, peeled and seeded
1 tablespoon garlic syrup
Juice of ½ lemon
Stevia to taste
6 ice cubes

Purée in a blender until smooth. Serve immediately.

Lung Cleanser
Serves 1

This healing smoothie helps to clear the lungs after that nasty cold. Try it and you'll be amazed at how much easier you breathe.

1 cup mango juice
1 cup frozen or fresh mango pieces
Juice of ½ lime
½ cup crushed ice or 3 ice cubes

Purée in a blender until smooth. Serve immediately.

Watermelon Cooler
Serves 1

On a hot summer day when only something cooling and refreshing will do, try this simple but delicious smoothie designed by Mother Nature.

2 cups ice-cold watermelon, peeled and seeded

Place in a blender and purée until smooth.

Raspberry Leaf Smoothie

Serves 1

This fruity, refreshing drink is beneficial for strengthening a woman's reproductive system . . . plus, it tastes fabulous!

½ cup raspberry leaf tea (brewed)
½ cup apple juice
1 cup frozen raspberries
Stevia to taste

Purée in a blender until smooth. Serve immediately.

Body-Mind Soother

Serves 1

This particular combination of ingredients is known for having a stabilizing effect on the nervous system while also aiding memory and concentration. It's a drink for your body and for your mind!

1 cup rice milk
1 tablespoon raw almonds
6 pitted dates
1 teaspoon ground ginger
½ teaspoon cinnamon

Purée in a blender until smooth.

Energizing Pick-Me-Up
Serves 1

This tasty, energy-boosting drink is the perfect way to start your day in lieu of breakfast. Or, whip it up in the late afternoon for a satisfying snack.

½ cup rice milk
½ cup yogurt
½ teaspoon vanilla extract
3 dried apricots, soaked in water
A handful of red seedless grapes
2 tablespoons walnuts
1 tablespoon wheat or oat bran
¼ teaspoon cinnamon
¼ teaspoon cardamom
Stevia to taste

Purée in a blender until smooth.

Cooling Cucumber Yogurt
Serves 1

This is the perfect cool, creamy treat for a hot day when your appetite is low but your urge to snack is high. The cucumber helps to cool the body while the yogurt provides a soothing texture and satisfies your hunger.

½ cup vegetable stock or water
3 scallions, chopped
1 cucumber, peeled and diced
Juice of 1 lemon
½ cup plain yogurt
A handful of fresh mint leaves, chopped

Combine ingredients in a blender and purée until smooth. Garnish with extra mint leaves.

Cream of Vegetable
Serves 1

Beta-carotene, protein, and the cleansing properties of cucumber all add up to a treat for your body. This works well as a light meal or afternoon snack when you will be having a late dinner engagement.

1 cup fresh carrot juice   *Juice of 1 lemon*
½ cup silken tofu   *½ cucumber, peeled and seeded*

Purée in a blender until smooth.

Chapter 6

Low-Carb Smoothies

Scientific research has shown that one of the leading causes of heart disease and cancer is obesity. This link is related to the deterioration of the American diet and the proliferation of high-fat foods and fast-food meals. Type II diabetes, once found only in the adult population, is becoming more and more common among children and teenagers as they overconsume sugar and refined food products. This problem has given rise to the popularity of a number of diets that bring about weight loss by reducing the amount of carbohydrates in the diet and balancing the right amounts of protein, carbohydrate, and fats in a given meal. In these diets, not all carbohydrates are acceptable, and the amounts of protein and fat are strictly regulated to ensure the body is not producing an overabundance of insulin, thus creating unwanted fat cells. With carbohydrate restriction differing between diets, however, it's difficult to keep up with what you can and cannot eat.

There was a time in the evolution of the human being when we needed the extra layers of fat to protect us from the cold and damp while living in caves and outside dwellings. Full-figured women were considered beautiful for their round, ample bodies and were chosen by suitors because they were thought to be the most fertile of the tribe. Maintaining a certain amount of fat on the body was a matter of survival for the species. Today, however, we live under very different circumstances. Much of our time is spent sitting in cars, at desks, and watching television, with a bit of walking in between. Health books and experts make huge amounts of money telling the American public how to eat, drink, and exercise and yet still the girth widens.

The Eastern philosophy of holistic living is to create balance in the body, which means learning to combine foods in ways that allow for a focus on vegetables, fruits, protein, fats, and dairy, with a moderate amount of grains and no refined food products. This is where supplementing a meal or snack with a low-carb smoothie can aid in the loss of extra weight and help to keep you healthy at the same time. Science has proved that the key to longevity and good health is eating less rather than more. What better way than to drink your meal with nutrients that give you what you need to sustain your energy for up to three hours?

Carbohydrates are simple sugars that we need to feed the body, primarily the brain. Our brain demands more blood supply than any other organ in the body, and what it feeds on is glucose, or sugar, which the body converts from—you guessed it—carbohydrates. The human body has an amazing natural intelligence that is structured to do one thing only and that is to survive. It is programmed to remember when fat was needed to be stored for famine times, for days of hard labor working in the fields or hunting a wild animal over long distances. Although we are more sedentary in today's world, we still need carbohydrates to provide the essential sugars to run our bodies. The trouble comes when we ingest too much of these sugars, leaving the body no choice but to store them as fat. Plain and simple. If you have provided your body with enough of what it needs during the day and then decide to have some fat-free fruit as a late-night snack, that carbohydrate/sugar can be turned to fat because you are lying in bed, sleeping, rather than burning it off with exercise.

The glycemic index gauges the speed with which a carbohydrate enters the bloodstream. Carbohydrates are comprised of three common sugars: fructose, which is found in fruits; glucose, whose primary sources are bread, pasta, vegetables, grains, cereals, and starches; and galactose, which is derived from dairy products. These three sugars are absorbed by the liver to be released into the bloodstream, but it is glucose that the liver dumps right into the blood, causing a sharp rise in blood sugar levels. In response, the pancreas takes action and secretes insulin to bring down those high blood sugar levels while telling the body to store the unneeded sugar as fat. Pretty smart, eh?

The amount of fiber in a food can make a big differ-ence in the rate in which the liver releases sugar. This is why fruits and vegetables are known to have a lower glycemic index and are considered appropriate carbohy-drates when creating a balanced diet. However, the thing to remember is that most fruits and their juices have a notoriously high carbohydrate count, which will just not do for those following a low-carbohydrate diet plan. The fruits used in the Low-Carb Smoothie recipes have a lower carbohydrate gram count and are safer to use while following your diet plan. You will also find many acceptable recipes in Chapter 2, Smoothies for Health, providing you with a wide variety from which to choose. On the supermarket shelves you can also find a number of low-carbohydrate, high-protein powders that can be added to your smoothie recipes. Make sure, however, to account for any extra sweetener and adjust accordingly.

Coconut Macadamia Indulgence
Serves 1

As if coconut and macadamia aren't wonderful enough in the same drink! Take this recipe over the top by adding a scoop of cocoa powder for a little extra kick.

½ cup soy milk
¼ cup light coconut milk
2 tablespoons unsweetened coconut flakes
⅓ cup unsalted macadamia nuts
½ cup crushed ice

Purée in a blender until smooth.

Low-Carb Fruit Smoothie

Serves 1

This simple combination of protein and vitamin C is the perfect low-carb solution for breakfast, lunch, or a snack.

1 cup water
¼ cup silken tofu
1 cup frozen strawberries
Stevia to taste
1 teaspoon vanilla extract (glycerin base)

Purée in a blender until smooth. Serve immediately.

Flavor Extracts

When using flavor extracts such as vanilla or almond, make sure they are nonalcoholic and glycerin based for the best results. Alcohol can interfere with the burning of fat in the body, so limit its use wherever you can.

Low-Carb Chocolate Smoothie

Serves 1

The dessert that eats like a meal! All the decadence of a dessert without having to break your diet.

1 cup water
¼ cup silken tofu
2 tablespoons cocoa powder
3 frozen strawberries
Stevia to taste
½ cup crushed ice

Purée in a blender until smooth. Serve immediately.

Gram Counts

Since you are counting grams of carbohydrates, you should know that 1 cup of half-and-half yields 10.4 grams of carbohydrates; whipping cream yields 6.64 grams; and silken tofu, 5 grams.

Cream Deluxe

Serves 1

This delectable recipe may be a forbidden treat for most, but it's a perfect concoction for a low-carb meal plan.

½ cup water
½ cup fresh cream
4 frozen strawberries
1 teaspoon banana extract (glycerin base)
Stevia to taste
½ cup crushed ice (optional)

Purée in a blender until smooth. Serve immediately.

Chocolate Cream Pudding

Serves 1

A chocolate lover's delight and the perfect treat for the low-carb dieter. Rich, thick, silky, and smooth—sip this baby really slowly. It's so good, you won't want it to end!

1 cup half-and-half
1 tablespoon cocoa powder
Stevia to taste
1 cup crushed ice

Purée until smooth, Serve immediately.

Creamy Coffee Delight

Serves 1

Jump-start your day the low-carb way. Morning can't come soon enough when this rise-and-shine treat is waiting for you.

½ cup brewed coffee
½ cup half-and-half
Stevia to taste
¼ teaspoon cinnamon

1 teaspoon vanilla
  extract (glycerin base)
1 cup crushed ice

Purée in a blender until smooth. Serve immediately.

The Story on Soy

Soy milk and tofu are both excellent sources of protein and are also low in carbohydrates. Half a cup of silken tofu yields 2 grams of carbohydrates, while 1 cup of soy milk yields 5 grams. Soy milk is made from cooked soy beans that have been pressed to remove the liquid, which is high in nutrients and protein. It is important to read the label on the soy milk package to check the amount and quality of sugars being used, as often these additives will raise the carbohydrate count past the acceptable amount. Once the soy container has been opened, it will last from five to ten days in the refrigerator.

Peaches and Cream

Serves 2

Thick and creamy with a tang of peaches and the richness of a milk shake, this smoothie delivers a good balance of protein, carbs, and omega-3 fatty acids.

>   *½ cup soy milk*
>   *½ cup silken tofu*
>   *1 cup frozen peach slices*
>   *½ teaspoon vanilla extract (glycerin base)*
>   *Stevia to taste*
>   *1½ teaspoons flax seed oil*

Purée in a blender until smooth.

Blueberries and Cream

Serves 2

The subtle blueberry flavor makes this a calming drink to help you get through a stressful morning, or provides a protein boost to fuel you for a long afternoon.

>   *½ cup soy milk*   *Stevia to taste*
>   *1 cup frozen blueberries*   *2 teaspoons flax seed oil*
>   *½ cup silken tofu*   *1 tablespoon protein*
>   *powder*

Purée in a blender until smooth.

Almond Delight

Serves 1

A fantastic low-carb drink! This delectable combination tastes so good, and it's packed with even more nutrients than spreading almond butter on an apple. Enjoy!

> ½ cup soy milk
> 1 large tablespoon almond butter
> 1 teaspoon vanilla extract (glycerin base)
> 1 apple, cored and sliced

Purée in a blender until smooth.

Cranberry Cream Delight

Serves 1

If you like a little pucker with your drink, then this tart treat is for you. However, if tangy isn't your style, add a little more Stevia to satisfy those taste buds.

> ⅓ cup unsweetened cranberry juice
> ⅓ cup water
> ½ cup silken tofu
> 1 cup frozen cherries
> Stevia to taste

Purée in a blender until smooth.

Chapter 7

Coffee, Tea, and Chai Smoothies

For centuries, enjoying a fine cup of tea or coffee during the day has been a time-honored tradition in cultures around the world. In Asia, sacred ceremonies are performed around the art of making the perfect cup of tea, while in Ethiopia, where coffee is said to have originated, wild coffee trees grow on the hillsides of Kaffa and Harar. There, it is served at the end of a meal, unsweetened, spiced then boiled and reboiled until it becomes a rich concentrate that has the faint smell of cloves.

All across the European continent, the pleasure of a good cup of espresso, cappuccino, or café con leche is part of taking a break from the worries and stress of everyday work and chores. In America, we often use coffee and tea as stimulants to get us going in the morning and jump-start us out of our midafternoon energy slump. Too much of this can eventually exhaust the adrenal glands and make you feel more tired despite the constant intake of caffeine.

The good news is that research has shown that having a cup of coffee a day is not harmful for the body, and it is the heavy cream and sugar that burden the body with the extra calories and fat grams. So, have that morning cup of java and try green tea for your afternoon beverage. The compounds found in green tea can protect against cancer, especially lung cancer. These compounds, known as catechins, have antibacterial properties that help to fight against tooth decay and gum disease. Green tea contains about half the amount of caffeine found in coffee and is also sold decaffeinated.

Long before the West woke up to a cup of brewed coffee, the ancient yogis of India created the exotic blend of black tea, cardamom, ginger, black pepper, cloves, and cinnamon that has come to be known as chai. Used to awaken the body to the new day, sharpen the mind with alertness, and stimulate the soul, this 5,000-year-old beverage can be used in much the same way as it was used by the holy men of India. Allow time to let the chai steep to obtain the fullest, richest taste and maximum energizing properties.

The South American tea yerba maté is known as the Green Gold of the Indios and is used as a whole-body tonic and energizer. A medicinal use of the leaves helps to clean the blood, tone the nervous system, and stimulate the brain. It's a good coffee or black tea substitute for those who want a shot in the arm without the harsh jolt of caffeine.

What better than to combine the flavor of coffee or your favorite tea with other healthful ingredients and create a beverage that can give you the stimulation and taste you are looking for? In this chapter you will find a variety of recipes using green tea, fruit tea, chai, and coffee to give you an alternative to that same old cup of morning brew. Feel free to use decaffeinated coffee and tea–the taste will still be the same.

Tea and Chai Smoothies

Frozen Chai Surprise
Serves 1

Decadent, indulgent, and surprising, consisting of spices and exotic flavors. Sip slowly, otherwise, this fantastic drink disappears much too soon!

1 cup prepared chai tea
3 scoops vanilla ice cream
½ large banana
1 teaspoon vanilla
Stevia to taste

Purée in a blender until smooth. Garnish with a sprig of mint.

Bananas Again?

When used in the recipes, bananas can be frozen or freshly peeled. Frozen will yield a thicker, richer smoothie, more along the lines of a milk shake.

Chocolate Chai Smoothie

Serves 1

Delicious, this unique combination of flavors provides a kick that will get you moving.

1 cup prepared chai
3–4 scoops chocolate ice cream
1 teaspoon vanilla
⅛ teaspoon cinnamon

Purée in a blender until smooth. Garnish with chocolate shavings.

Thick, Thicker, Thickest

The proper thickness for the perfect smoothie can be an individual's preference. More fruit, particularly frozen, will add thickness, as will the addition of ice cubes or crushed ice. Yogurt or ice cream will fill out a thin concoction, but for those who prefer a smoothie with more flow, decreasing the amount of whole fruits will do the trick.

Apple Pie Smoothie
Serves 1

Although it may be your favorite part of the pie, you will not miss the crust while sipping this delightful combination.

1 cup prepared soy chai tea
1 teaspoon vanilla extract
⅛ teaspoon cinnamon
¼ cup raisins, soaked in water
½ small apple, peeled and cored
½ cup crushed ice

Purée in a blender until smooth. Serve immediately.

Santa Goes South

Serves 1

Serve this mildly spiced smoothie any time of year, but it works especially well as a crowd-pleasing Christmas nog during the holiday season.

1 cup prepared soy chai
1 teaspoon vanilla extract
⅛ teaspoon cinnamon
¼ cup raisins, soaked in water
½ small apple, peeled and cored
3 dates
½ large banana
½ cup crushed ice

Purée in a blender until smooth. Serve immediately.

Spicy Chai

Chai tea can be a combination of black tea, spices, sweeteners, and milk or soy milk. When making chai tea from scratch, use ¾ cup of brewed chai tea, ⅓ cup of soy or dairy milk, and add honey to taste (usually 2 teaspoons). The combination of ingredients is your choice, but for the following recipes, ice cream can be interpreted as dairy or nondairy and chai tea as caffeinated or decaffeinated.

Green Tea Smoothie

Serves 1

Did you know that green tea could taste this good and still be good for you? Enjoy this tasty recipe as a complement to your favorite breakfast or lunch.

2 Japanese green tea bags
½ cup boiling water
3–4 crushed cardamom pods
     or ¼–½ teaspoon cardamom powder
1 cup crushed ice
1 cup vanilla soy milk
2 tablespoons honey

1. Steep the tea bags in the boiling water for ten minutes
2. Add cardamom. Stir. Allow the tea mixture to cool.
3. In a blender, combine the green tea mixture with crushed ice, vanilla soy milk, and honey. Purée until smooth. Garnish with a sprig of mint.

Island Spice Smoothie
Serves 1

The refreshing, complex flavors of this drink are pleasing to the palate, with a subtle and lingering aftertaste. Very nice.

Syrup:
½ cup brewed lemon tea
2 tablespoons cane sugar
10 cloves
2 cinnamon sticks crushed or ½ teaspoon cinnamon

Boil until reduced to ⅓ cup; cool.

Smoothie base:
1 cup crushed ice
1 cup pineapple juice (or orange juice)
2 teaspoons lemon juice
⅓ cup prepared syrup

In a blender, combine smoothie base ingredients. Purée until smooth. Serve immediately.

Mango Chai Zip

Serves 2

A surprise for the taste buds and a surefire way to boost your energy for a hectic day.

½ cup mango juice
½ cup brewed chai tea
¼ cup silken tofu
½ cup frozen peaches
Juice of ½ lemon
Stevia to taste or 1 tablespoon honey

Purée in a blender until smooth. Serve immediately.

Lemon and Tofu

Here is a great marriage of two foods that need each other. The lemon's tartness is softened by the creamy tofu, while the slight bean taste of the tofu is transformed by the fresh lemon juice to a flavor reminiscent of cream or yogurt.

Amazon Energy Booster

Serves 1

Yerba maté is a great way to boost your energy without the negative effects of a caffeine high.

½ cup papaya juice
½ cup brewed yerba maté tea
½ cup frozen papaya pieces
¼ cup silken tofu
Juice of ½ lemon
Stevia to taste

Purée in a blender until smooth. Serve immediately.

Fresh Lemon Juice versus Bottled

No doubt about it, fresh beats bottled hands down for taste, tartness, and nutrition. It's worth the time it takes to cut a lemon in half and press it against the lemon juicer. You'll be happy you took the time.

Green Tea–Apple Surprise

Serves 1

An apple a day keeps the doctor way, and a Green Tea-Apple Surprise smoothie, loaded with antioxidants and phytochemicals, is sure to keep you healthy all season long.

½ cup apple juice
½ cup green tea, brewed
½ cup frozen peeled apple slices
2 tablespoons frozen vanilla yogurt
Stevia to taste

Purée in a blender until smooth. Serve immediately.

Mocha Peanut Supreme

Serves 1

Get your coffee and your protein all in one shot. This recipe is a bit of an indulgence, but oh, so good.

¾ cup strong coffee
3–4 scoops vanilla ice cream
1 tablespoon peanut butter
1 tablespoon honey
½ cup crushed ice

Purée in a blender until smooth. Serve immediately.

Coffee Smoothie Recipes

It would almost seem that the favorite national pastime of countries worldwide is the appreciation of a good cup of joe in the morning. In most towns and large cities, there are whole stores dedicated to the sale of coffees from all over the world. Supermarkets carry a large variety of brands and flavors, and having the right coffee machine is critical to the true coffee connoisseur. From espresso, to black drip, to French roast with cream and sugar, there are endless combinations when using the dark, rich liquid from the coffee bean. Whether it is that first cup in the morning or the after-dinner drink with the addition of a fine liqueur, the following recipes will be sure to give you a new appreciation for that cup of java. Allow the coffee to cool before using it in these recipes.

Mocha Java Smoothie
Serves 1

Combine your breakfast with your coffee for a real treat. For a thicker recipe, add 2 tablespoons vanilla yogurt.

¾ cup brewed dark coffee
½ cup soy/rice milk
2–3 tablespoons
    maple syrup
1 banana, peeled

1½ tablespoons cocoa
    powder
1 teaspoon vanilla
6 ice cubes

Place all ingredients in a blender and purée until smooth.

Heavenly Twins

Serves 1

Your taste buds will sing once you try this unique East-meets-West recipe—what a burst of flavor!

¾ cup strong French roast coffee
½ cup soy chai
1 teaspoon vanilla
⅛ teaspoon cinnamon
2 teaspoons cane sugar
½ cup crushed ice

Purée in a blender until smooth. Serve immediately.

Chocolate Chai

Serves 1

Different, defiant, and delicious, this recipe sure satisfies that chocolate craving.

¾ cup strong coffee
½ cup milk
1 teaspoon vanilla
1 tablespoon plus 1 teaspoon cocoa powder
1–2 tablespoons maple syrup
½ cup crushed ice

Purée in a blender until smooth. Serve immediately.

Cocoa Mocha
Serves 2

If you are a chocolate and coconut lover, you'll love this tasty treat.

¾ cup strong coffee
½ cup milk
1 teaspoon vanilla
⅓ cup unsweetened coconut milk
1–2 tablespoons maple syrup (or to taste)
1 tablespoon plus 1 teaspoon cocoa powder
½ cup crushed ice

Purée in a blender until smooth. Serve immediately.

Almond Hazelnut Cream
Serves 1

After a fine meal and a light dessert, only this cup of coffee will do! This delightful concoction, blended with liqueur and ice, is a sensational taste treat.

1 ounce amaretto
½ ounce Frangelico
1 cup black coffee
2 ounces cream
½ cup crushed ice

Purée in a blender until smooth.

Almond Cocoa Mocha

Serves 2

This nutty chocolate recipe is sure to satisfy that after-noon snack attack!

¾ cup strong coffee
½ cup milk
1 teaspoon vanilla
⅓ cup unsweetened coconut milk
3 tablespoons maple syrup (or to taste)
1 tablespoon plus 1 teaspoon cocoa powder
1 tablespoon roasted almond butter
½ cup crushed ice

Purée in a blender until smooth. Serve immediately

Hazelnut Coffee

Serves 1

The subtle nuttiness of the hazelnuts makes this the per-fect evening treat, whatever the occasion.

1½ ounces Frangelico
½ ounce dark crème de cacao
½ cup black coffee
2 ounces heavy cream
½ ounce crushed ice

Purée in a blender until smooth.

Mocha Peanut Chocolate Deluxe

Serves 1

Put it all together for a taste treat so thick and rich that you can eat it with a spoon.

¾ cup strong coffee
3–4 scoops chocolate ice cream
1½ tablespoons peanut butter
1 tablespoon honey
½ banana
1 teaspoon vanilla
1 tablespoon cocoa powder (optional, for dark
    chocolate)
½ cup crushed ice

Purée in a blender until smooth. Serve immediately.

Brandy Dandy

Serves 1

This isn't your mother's milk shake! Add a kick to your coffee with this fun blender drink.

2 ounces brandy
½ cup black coffee
2 scoops vanilla ice cream

Purée in a blender until smooth.

Carob Coffee

Serves 2

A fine substitute for chocolate, carob cuts down on the caffeine and the calories.

1 cup brewed coffee
1 cup carob milk
3 tablespoons yogurt
1 banana
½ teaspoon almond extract
1–2 tablespoons maple syrup
1 cup crushed ice

Purée in a blender until smooth.

Coffee Cacao

Serves 1

Coffee, chocolate, and ice cream all together . . . it really doesn't get any better than this!

½ cup crème de cacao
½ cup black coffee
1½ scoops coffee ice cream

Purée in a blender until smooth.

Chapter 8

Party Smoothies

The invitations have gone out, the food menu has been planned, and the bar is stocked and ready to go. No matter what the occasion, smoothies are the perfect addition to any party, whether blended with ice cream and your favorite liqueurs to make thick, creamy shakes, or fruit juice and crushed ice to make flavorful slushes.

Drawing from standard recipes of classic drinks, these recipes for Party Smoothies put a new twist on an old theme. The Highball, the shaken and stirred cocktail, and many more can be transformed with the help of a blender, crushed ice, and a little imagination. However, what updates many of these classics is the exciting addition—and new combinations—of fresh fruit and vegetable juices, whole fruits, and ice cream.

While prepared drink mixes are convenient and easy to use, it is always better to start from scratch using the highest quality ingredients available. Fresh lemon, lime, and orange juices are far superior to bottled concentrates, while whole fruit can be either fresh or frozen. Here again, the quality of the ingredients can have much to do with the outcome of taste and, in some cases, with beating that morning hangover. Replacing sugar with Stevia, for example, can help in reducing the size of your headache, while having water and something salty can help rebalance the body's chemistry and ease the agony of alcohol withdrawal. When drinking alcoholic beverages, consider the maxim "all things in moderation"—particularly since you are dealing with a very powerful drug that can influence how you judge situations, coordinate your body and mind, and perceive what is going on around you.

Margaritas, daiquiris, and coladas are all fruit-based drinks that have been inspired by tropical nights and long hot days in the sun. The creation of the daiquiri came about completely by accident, sometime around the turn of the century, when, during an outbreak of malaria in the town of Daiquiri, Cuba, it was discovered that rum was the only way to bring down the malarial fever. Combining it with lime juice and sugar to make it more palatable for the patient, the doctors inadvertently discovered a drink that would become famous the world over.

The margarita originated in Mexico and features smooth, pale gold tequila made from the blue agave plant, a member of the cactus family.

The Caribbean colada marries the creaminess of coconut with the sweetness of rum, which is extracted from sugar cane and weighs in at 80 proof alcohol. It's strong enough to have you singing the old school anthem after a few drinks, but so delicious you will consider it dessert in a glass. Fresh fruit such as banana, pineapple, or strawberries can be added for a change of flavor and variety. Using unsweetened coconut milk allows you to control the amount of sugar that goes into your colada, but there is also a sweetened version available in most grocery stores.

The new variations on these recipes found in this chapter are sure to kick any get-together into high gear. Fruit-based drinks are inspired by the natural abundance and variety found in the tropics and team rum, fresh fruit, and juice with crushed ice. These delicious drinks can also be prepared without alcohol—just substitute an extra splash of juice or add a few more pieces of fruit.

Frozen Blizzard

Serves 1

An excellent treat to enjoy on those hot summer nights! To cut down on the dairy, substitute soy milk if you so choose.

> ½ cup milk
> 1 ounce Kahlúa
> 1 ounce vodka
> 1 cup crushed ice

Purée in a blender until smooth.

Yelping for More
Serves 1

Start with brewed coffee and allow it to cool before adding it to this wonderful pick-me-up. This tastes more like dessert than a drink, but it packs a nice punch. Have too many and you'll be getting picked up off the floor.

½ ounce Grand Marnier
½ ounce Irish cream liqueur
½ ounce coffee liqueur
½ cup brewed coffee
1 cup crushed ice

Purée in a blender until smooth.

Frozen Strawquiri
Serves 1

The Stevia helps to regulate blood sugar levels, which can prevent that troublesome morning-after hangover.

1 cup strawberries
1–2 ounces rum
Juice of ½ lime
Stevia to taste
1 cup crushed ice

Purée in a blender until smooth.

The Scotsman

Serves 1

For the traditionalist who wants a slight change of pace without adding any other ingredients. Plain and simple— scotch and rocks.

> *2 ounces scotch* *1 cup crushed ice*

> Purée in a blender until smooth.

Almond Scot

Serves 1

This smoothie is for the bonny lass who likes a hint of almond to sweeten her drink.

> *1½ ounces scotch* *1 cup crushed ice*
> *¾ ounce amaretto*

> Purée in a blender until smooth.

Black Jack

Serves 1

Somewhere in Scotland there must have been a man called Black Jack, and so here's to him wandering the Highlands still wearing the kilt.

> *1½ ounces scotch* *1 cup crushed ice*
> *1 ounce coffee brandy*

> Purée in a blender until smooth.

Loghaire Long Hair

Serves 1

Scotch blended with a hint of bitters—for lads and lassies with sophisticated palates.

2 ounces scotch
1 teaspoon water
½ teaspoon sugar
Dash of bitters
Zest of ½ lemon
1 cup crushed ice

Purée in a blender until smooth.

Through the Wall

Serves 1

Looking for a change of pace when out with friends? Try this refreshing taste sensation.

1 ounce scotch
1 ounce blue curaçao
½ ounce peach-flavored brandy
3 ounces grapefruit juice
½ ounce lemon juice
½ cup crushed ice

Purée in a blender until smooth.

Passion

Serves 1

Picture yourself on a Caribbean beach, the balmy breeze soft against your bare arms, the love of your life walking toward you, arm extended, offering you the nectar of the gods.

½ cup mango juice   *½ ounce rum*
½ cup papaya juice   *½ ounce Midori*
½ ounce tequila   *½ cup crushed ice*

Purée in a blender until smooth.

Bloody Mary

Serves 1

Predinner cocktail or next morning's hair of the dog, this one is an all-American classic.

½ cup tomato juice
1 ripe tomato, seeded and peeled
1 stalk raw celery
1 teaspoon horseradish
1½ ounces vodka
Dash Tabasco
Juice of ½ lemon
Salt and pepper to taste

Purée in a blender until smooth.

Grasshopper Pie

Serves 1

Grasshopper cocktails are traditionally made with crème de menthe, so for variations, change cacao to Galliano, amaretto, or blackberry brandy.

2 ounces cream
½ ounce crème de menthe
1 ounce crème de cacao
2 scoops vanilla ice cream

Purée in a blender until smooth.

Miami Beach

Serves 1

Dead of winter, no sign of the sun, looking pale and pasty—pop that salsa CD into the player, put on your favorite swimwear, and with a simple whirr of the blender, South Beach comes to you.

¾ cup grapefruit juice
¼ cup unsweetened coconut milk
Juice of ½ lemon
1–2 tablespoons sweetener
1 cup crushed ice

Purée in a blender until smooth.

Going South

Serves 1

Part orange smoothie, part Southern charm, this drink is sure to become the hit of any party!

1 ounce gin
1 ounce kirshwasser
1 ounce Cointreau
½ cup orange juice
1 teaspoon lemon juice
½ cup crushed ice

Purée in a blender until smooth.

Bourbon Freeze

Serves 1

Ever notice how some people like their bourbon, some their scotch, and some don't like anything? If you've picked this recipe, guess we know what you like best.

2 ounces bourbon
1 cup pineapple juice
½ cup pineapple pieces
½ cup crushed ice

Purée in a blender until smooth.

Cranberry Cocktail

Serves 1

This drink is tart and tingling to the taste buds. Make sure to blend to a fine consistency for the best possible effect, and garnish with a sprig of mint.

2 ounces bourbon
⅔ cup cranberry juice (sweetened)
½ ounce lime juice
½ ounce grenadine
⅔ cup crushed ice

Purée in a blender until smooth.

Happy Go Lucky

Serves 1

This is definitely not a substitute for a healthy smoothie, although it sure tastes like one. For added thickness and extra nutrients, add a ripe banana to the mix.

2 ounces brandy
1 ounce crème de banana
⅔ cup orange juice
1 teaspoon lemon juice
½ cup crushed ice

Purée in a blender until smooth.

The Hyper Russian

Serves 1

A rich, frosty shot in the arm that will have you up and dancing in no time. Who knew smoothies could be this much fun?

1½ ounces vodka
½ ounce coffee liqueur
½ ounce cream or soy creamer
½ cup crushed ice

Purée in a blender until smooth.

Welcome to the Islands

Serves 1

Even without the rum, this drink helps get any group in the mood for a tropical party. Cool, sweet, and refreshing, it's the perfect poolside libation.

2 ounces rum
½ cup fresh orange juice
½ cup fresh grapefruit juice
1 teaspoon lemon juice
1 ripe banana
¾ cup crushed ice

Purée in a blender until smooth.

Red-Faced Russian

Serves 1

Take a little bit of vodka, a little bit of vitamin C, and add a little cream to make it oh, so smooth. . . .

1 ounce strawberry liquor
6 frozen strawberries
1 ounce vodka
1 ounce cream or soy creamer

Purée in a blender until smooth.

Crème for a Day

When a recipe calls for crème, you can substitute a soy-based coffee creamer in its place. Account for the extra sugar in the creamer by using less in the recipe; otherwise, you can trade one for one.

That Healing Daiquiri

Serves 1

When the malarial fever hit Cuba, this is what was created to stop it cold. Okay, so you don't have malaria, but it will still make you feel pretty good.

> *2 ounces light rum*
> *¼ cup lime juice*
> *8 ounces water*
> *Stevia to taste*
> *½ cup crushed ice*

Purée in a blender until smooth.

Peachy Rum Daiquiri

Serves 1

This luscious drink is fun to the max and feeds your body at the same time. Perfect for a Saturday afternoon surprise!

> *2 ounces light rum*
> *½ ounce peach-flavored brandy*
> *Juice of ½ lime*
> *½ cup frozen peach slices*
> *Stevia to taste*
> *½ cup crushed ice*

Purée in a blender until smooth.

Cuban Pineapple

Serves 1

The perfect marriage of ingredients to shake things up a bit! The flavors dance together on your tongue like a sexy Cuban mambo.

2 ounces rum
½ ounce triple sec
Juice of ½ lime
½ cup pineapple pieces
Stevia to taste
½ cup crushed ice

Purée in a blender until smooth.

Banana Lime Daiquiri

Serves 1

For a thicker, richer daiquiri, use a frozen banana and reduce the amount of crushed ice.

2 ounces rum
½ ounce triple sec
Juice of ½ lime
1 ripe banana
½ cup crushed ice

Purée in a blender until smooth.

Mocha Russian

Serves 1

This recipe really is the milk shake that has more! The perfect combination of an after-dinner drink and dessert all in one.

1 ounce coffee liqueur
1 ounce vodka
2 scoops chocolate ice cream

Purée in a blender until smooth.

Layer Perfect

Place the ingredients into the blender in the following order: alcohol, juice, sugar, fruit, and crushed ice. This way, you are ensured the proper blending of ingredients, making for the perfect smoothie.

Orange Rum Frappe

Serves 1

Whipped up and ready to go, this recipe is great with the rum, but try it without for a fast pick-me-up.

1½ ounces light rum
½ cup fresh orange juice
½ ripe banana
½ cup crushed ice

Purée in a blender until smooth.

Making Waves

Serves 1

If you serve this drink at your next summertime get-together, you're sure to make a big splash!

½ ounce vodka
½ ounce rum
½ ounce gin
½ ounce triple sec
½ ounce grenadine
2 ounces pineapple juice
1 ounce cranberry juice
1 cup crushed ice

Purée in a blender until smooth.

Apples and Rum

Serves 1

Light, sweet, and with a taste of apples, this smoothie is perfect as is, but add a whole ripe apple, sliced and cored, and your body will thank you.

1½ ounces light rum
Juice of ½ lime
½ cup apple juice
½ ounce calvados
Stevia to taste
1 cup crushed ice

Purée in a blender until smooth.

Just What Is a Frappe?

According to Webster's dictionary, a frappe is a dessert drink made of partly frozen fruit juices or a beverage poured over shaved ice.

Piña Colada

Serves 1

A favorite of anyone who has ever visited the islands and fallen in love with the coconut palm trees swaying in the breeze. If this does not apply, try this recipe and you'll be booking a trip come morning.

2 ounces light rum   *½ cup pineapple juice*
2 ounces coconut cream   *½ cup crushed ice*

Purée in a blender until smooth.

Packs a Punch

Serves 1

If you've been searching for the perfect punch for your next big bash, look no further. This one has it all . . . and then some!

2 ounces dark rum   *2 ounces fresh orange juice*
1 ounce light rum   *2 ounces pineapple juice*
Juice of ½ lime   *½ cup pineapple pieces*
Juice of ½ lemon   *1 cup crushed ice*

Purée in a blender until smooth.

Almond Colada
Serves 1

Almonds, coconut, and pineapple have a soothing effect on the body that will have you putting your feet up to relax.

3 ounces amaretto
2 ounces coconut cream
⅓ cup pineapple juice
½ cup crushed ice

Purée in a blender until smooth.

Banana Colada
Serves 1

To substitute unsweetened coconut milk for the coconut cream, use Stevia powder or other sweetener according to your taste.

2 ounces light rum   *½ cup pineapple juice*
2 ounces coconut cream   *½ cup crushed ice*
1 ripe banana

Purée in a blender until smooth.

Banana Nectar

Serves 1

With or without the vodka, you won't want to miss this delectable drink. Apricots are considered by some to be "the fountain of youth," orange juice has vitamin C, bananas are loaded with potassium, and lemon is good for the liver. This is definitely a drink with benefits!

1 ounce vodka	*Juice of ½ lemon*
1 ounce apricot nectar	*½ banana*
½ cup fresh orange juice	*½ cup crushed ice*

Purée in a blender until smooth.

Strawberries and Rum

Serves 1

The colada all gussied up and ready to bring a smile to your face.

2 ounces rum
2 ounces coconut cream
6 frozen strawberries
½ cup pineapple juice
½ cup crushed ice

Purée in a blender until smooth.

The Basic Margarita
Serves 1

Down Mexico way, on a hot day in July, a smart bartender put this together and made his country famous.

2 ounces tequila	*Stevia to taste*
1 ounce triple sec	*1 cup crushed Ice*
2 ounces lime juice	*Salt to rim the glass*

Purée in a blender until smooth.

Strawberry Margarita
Serves 1

Strawberries give this version such a distinctive taste that many people will drink only margaritas prepared this way.

2 ounces tequila	*Stevia to taste*
1 ounce triple sec	*½ cup crushed ice*
3 ounces lime juice	*Salt to rim the glass*
½ cup frozen strawberries	

Purée in a blender until smooth. Garnish with a strawberry on the rim.

Coconut Melange

Serves 1

Just reading this recipe should make you want to go out and get all the ingredients, invite over a group of friends, and get the blender working.

2 ounces tequila
2 ounces milk
1 ounce coconut cream
3 ounces pineapple juice

½ ripe banana
½ cup frozen strawberries
½ cup crushed ice

Purée in a blender until smooth.

Cranberry Margarita

Serves 1

Cranberry is very beneficial to the body—here, it's combined with Stevia to balance blood sugar levels and tequila to raise them.

2 ounces tequila
Juice of ½ lime
2 ounces unsweetened cranberry juice
4 ounces water
Stevia to taste
1 cup crushed ice

Purée in a blender until smooth.

Cool Me Down
Serves 1

The cooling flavor of Midori is a wonderful addition to this combination of ingredients.

1 ounce Midori
½ ounce rum
½ ounce vodka
Juice of 1 lime

2 ounces grapefruit juice
½ cup orange juice
1 cup crushed ice

Purée in a blender until smooth.

Pitcher of Sangria
Serves 6

When friends come over, this is a wonderful recipe to serve with or without the crushed ice.

1 bottle dry red wine
2 ounces triple sec
2 ounces fresh
orange juice
Juice of ½ lemon

¼ cup sugar or Stevia
to taste
2 cups ice cubes

Purée in a blender until smooth.

The Finn
Serves 2

Sweet and bitter combine here to create something really special. For those beer drinkers who want their Guinness as a meal.

8 ounces Guinness beer
4 pitted dates
½ banana
½ cup oat milk
¼ cup unsweetened coconut

Pinch cinnamon
Stevia to taste
½ tablespoon protein powder
½ cup crushed ice

Purée in a blender until smooth.

Guinness for Lunch
Serves 2

Sacrilege, you say? Not after you have a go with this surprisingly delicious meal of Guinness and friends.

6 ounces Guinness beer
6 ounces apple juice
½ banana
¼ cup walnuts

6 whole cranberries
⅓ cup oats
½ cup crushed ice

Purée in a blender until smooth.

Guinness and Almonds

Serves 2

Strong, hearty, and loaded with taste, the almond butter gives a smoothness and flavor to this drink that will have you going back for another swallow.

8 ounces Guinness beer
4 dates
½ ripe banana
½ cup oat milk
¼ cup unsweetened
    coconut
Pinch cinnamon
1 teaspoon vanilla
1 tablespoon almond
    butter
Stevia to taste
½ cup crushed ice

Purée in a blender until smooth.

Irish Beer

Most famous is Guinness beer, with a deep dark color and a strong bitter taste that blends well with other ingredients. A powerful and strengthening addition to the growing list of smoothie possibilities.

Chapter 9

The Simply Smoothies Eating Plan

Once you have experienced the benefits of drinking your daily nutrients, you will want to incorporate a smoothie meal into your daily routine. The Simply Smoothies Eating Plan provides three separate week-by-week menus that can be followed one after the other or used as an independent diet program. Whether you are looking to lose weight by following a low-carb diet, want to increase your daily consumption of fruits and vegetables, or are just interested in doing a weekend juice fast, you need look no further to find the proper guidance. When you are feeling the need to cut back on rich, high-fat foods and want to take a few weeks to relax and cleanse your body, try following each menu plan for a week, then switch to the next, finally ending with a week of modifying your foods to include a higher percentage of raw and lightly steamed fruits and vegetables, which will prepare you for a short juice fast. Remember to always consult your doctor before going without solid food, particularly if you are taking prescription medication.

The Standard American Diet, known as SAD, can be

very stressful to the human body because of its reliance on refined flours, sugar, and hydrogenated fats. With the rise of obesity in this country, it may appear that the American public is getting plenty to eat and should feel satisfied at the end of a long working day. The truth is that because the SAD is made up of processed, chemical-laden, and overcooked meals, the body can be malnourished and instinctively continues to eat in an attempt to find some nourishment. Once a whole-foods diet is undertaken, cravings subside, energy is restored, and people find that they eat less because they are getting more nutrition in a moderate amount of food.

This chapter will outline three separate healthy eating plans designed to provide you with optimal nutrition without counting calories or fat grams. The Healthy Balance Week allows you to change your food choices one day at a time and replace them with beneficial oils and high-fiber and nutrient-dense alternatives. It is necessary to keep in mind that you should not take a food out of your diet without having something to put in its place. That means that if you love to eat bagels made with refined white flour, instead try sprouted whole-grain bagels, which you can find in the freezer section of your local health food store. Rather than using cream cheese on your bagel, go for some roasted almond butter and fruit-sweetened jam instead. These kinds of changes won't take you very far from what you are used to eating, and they provide your body with more health-packed ingredients. Weight loss may be gradual and slow depending on your intake of calories versus your energy output, meaning that exercise is an important part of any lifestyle plan.

The Low-Carb Week follows in the footsteps of many popular diet programs based on nutritional research that shows how eating a diet high in certain carbohydrates, such as breads, sugars, and grains, can cause weight gain. This does not mean that you will never again experience the joy of eating a warm slice of sourdough bread with butter, but it will limit your intake of these temptations to occasional meals. Since carbohydrates turn to sugar once digested by the body, too much of this needed sugar can be stored as fat, which can be very difficult to eliminate if your diet is made up of high amounts of carbohydrates. Try keeping a food diary for a week, writing down everything you eat and drink and the times of day that you have these foods. Don't try to eat "really well" that week, just follow your usual diet and keep a small notebook with you to write it all down. Then look over your list and consider the following questions:

- What foods make up the bulk of my diet? (Candy, breads, fruits, vegetables, cereals, protein, fried foods, etc.)
- What liquids do I drink the most? (Soda pop, diet soda, water, tea, coffee, fruit juice, etc.)
- What time of day do I eat the majority of my food? (Morning, afternoon, or evening.)
- How many servings of fruits and vegetables do I have in a day?

- Do I eat the same thing every day for breakfast, lunch, and dinner?
- How many times in a day do I eat foods containing sugar and/or caffeine?

Once you can see what you are putting into your body on a daily basis, you will have a better understanding of what you are eating too much or too little of, and you can begin to make the necessary changes. Eating according to the Low-Carb Week can help you to balance your intake of carbohydrates, proteins, and fats.

It has been written in ancient texts and scriptures, passed down from teachers to students, that the secret to a long healthy life is a flexible spine and a clean colon. This necessitates the consistent practice of eating organic whole foods, getting daily exercise, drinking pure water, and fasting periodically. The Cleansing Week is based on the principles of internal cleansing to ensure all the organs of elimination—the kidneys, the lungs, the large and small intestines, and the skin- function to their maximum potential, which is to efficiently break down, absorb, distribute, and eliminate the foods that come into the body. From the mouth to the anus is one long (thirty-foot) tube with a number of bends and turns, and food must follow this path before being released. Colon cancer is the number-one form of cancer in America, and that fact is partially due to our toxic, stressed, and overloaded bowels. Fasting allows the digestive system time to rest from the constant onslaught of food, and the body can then cleanse and rejuvenate the entire system.

The Healthy Balance Week

The Healthy Balance Week is an excellent way to make a transition from health-destroying foods to the highest quality ingredients available. Made up of whole grains, sprouted grain breads, natural sweeteners, legumes, fruits, and vegetables, this is a program you can adapt to very easily. Feel free to adapt the seven days of menus to extend into a second or even third week once you get the hang of what foods to buy and how to prepare them for your particular taste. Here are a few suggestions for setting up your daily eating program:

- Typically, lunch should be your main meal of the day, and dinner the lightest, since you are the least active at that time and preparing for a good night's sleep.
- Try to eat your animal protein either in the morning or at lunchtime, as it takes six to eight hours for the body to break down and digest it.
- Remember to drink your food and chew your liquids. Meaning, you should chew each mouthful in order to release the necessary digestive enzymes needed for digestion.
- So as not to dilute your digestive juices, drink liquids a half hour before meals and a half hour after meals, not with your meals.
- Never eat until you are full and your stomach is bulging. Leave room for digestion to occur in the stomach. Nothing moves if it is packed in too tightly.
- Try to finish eating each day by 7:30 P.M. to allow the

body plenty of time to digest, absorb, and rest before "breaking your fast," breakfast, the next morning.

- Save desserts for occasions such as birthdays, holidays, or nights out at a fancy restaurant. Instead, choose a smoothie from "Smoothies for Fun" or "Party Smoothies" to satisfy a nagging sweet tooth.
- Many of the traditional recipes that you use from day to day or week to week can easily be adapted to include organic whole-grain flours, fresh fruits and vegetables, as well as high-quality animal proteins.
- When making pancakes, use spelt or buckwheat flour instead of refined white flour. Substitute soy or rice milk for dairy milk, and buy real maple syrup instead of commercial corn syrup with artificial flavorings disguised to taste like the real thing.
- Lemon juice must be freshly squeezed for each serving for optimal benefits. Start with juicing half a lemon for your morning drink. If you want more you can always add what you need.
- Raw, unfiltered apple cider vinegar is very cleansing and alkaline-forming for the blood. You can use it to lose weight by having 1 teaspoon in 8 ounces of water with 1 teaspoon of honey or Stevia a half hour before meals.
- Take time each day to exercise, whether it's taking a quick walk in the afternoons, working out at the gym, or attending a yoga class on a regular basis.
- Keep your dinner meal simple, with an abundance of vegetables and beans, tofu, or tempeh (a fermented soy product) as your protein source.

The Simply Smoothies Eating Plan 171

Monday

Upon rising: Squeeze the juice of ½ lemon in 8 ounces of warm water and add Stevia to taste. (This prepares the digestive system for the day and helps to clean the liver.)

Breakfast: Choice of smoothie from Chapter 2, Smoothies for Health, or Chapter 7, Coffee, Tea, and Chai Smoothies

Snack: Piece of fruit with some live cultured yogurt

Lunch: Green salad, fish or organic chicken, balsamic vinaigrette

Snack: Roasted almonds and raisins

Dinner: Vegetable Stir-Fry with chickpeas or tofu, green salad with lemon vinaigrette

Snack: Air-popped popcorn

Vegetable Stir-Fry

Serves 2

1 tablespoon olive oil	*1 large zucchini, chopped*
½ large onion, chopped	*1 teaspoon dried basil*
2 cloves garlic, sliced	*1 teaspoon dried oregano*
1 carrot, chopped	*Salt to taste*
1 portobello mushroom, sliced	

1. In a large heavy skillet or wok, heat the oil and add the onion and garlic, cooking until tender, about 3 minutes.
2. Add the carrot, stir well, cover and cook for three more minutes. *(continued)*

3. Add the mushroom, zucchini, basil, oregano, and salt. Stir well, cover, and allow to cook, removing the cover every few minutes to stir the vegetables.
4. When tender but still crisp, remove from the heat and serve over brown rice or whole-grain pasta with a sprinkle of Parmesan cheese.

Tuesday

Upon rising: Lemon juice and water with Stevia
Breakfast: Oatmeal Delight 🥄
Snack: 1 orange
Lunch: Bowl of vegetable soup, green salad, and a sprouted whole-grain bagel topped with toasted almond butter
Snack: Choice of a smoothies from Chapter 3, Smoothies for Fun
Dinner: Grilled fish, broccoli sautéed with garlic, mixed vegetable salad

🥄 Oatmeal Delight

Serves 2

⅔ cup oatmeal (not instant)
¼ cup raisins
¼ cup sunflower seeds
Stevia to taste
2 cups water
¼ teaspoon cinnamon
½ teaspoon vanilla extract

1. Place ingredients in a medium saucepan, cover, and allow to soak overnight. *(continued)*

2. In the morning, cook over medium heat until water is absorbed and cereal is heated through.
3. Serve with a choice of flax seed oil, butter, maple syrup, yogurt, or milk.

Yogurt

Yogurt is now made with soy or rice as an alternative to dairy brands and still contains the good probiotics that you get from the dairy varieties.

Wednesday

Upon rising: Unsweetened cranberry juice with water and Stevia

Breakfast: Quick-and-Easy Omelet 🍲, whole-grain toast, and organic butter

Snack: 1 apple

Lunch: Sandwich made with whole-grain bread, avocado, tofu or chicken, lettuce, with mayonnaise or mustard (optional); side of baked blue corn chips (no hydrogenated oils)

Snack: Choice of a smoothie from Chapter 4, Exotic Fruit Smoothies

Dinner: East India Curry Dish 🍲 served over brown rice

🍲 Quick-and-Easy Omelet

Serves 2

2 tablespoons water
½ bag frozen leaf spinach
4 organic eggs   *(continued)*

1 teaspoon dried dill
Salt to taste
¼ cup goat's milk feta cheese, crumbled

1. In a heavy skillet heat the water and add the spinach, stirring well to defrost. Cover and lower heat to low.
2. Meanwhile, break the eggs into a medium-size bowl and whisk to combine. Add the dill and salt, stirring well.
3. Remove the cover from the skillet, stir the spinach and add the egg mixture, moving the pan to evenly distribute the eggs. Top with the feta cheese, re-cover, and allow to cook until the eggs have set up.
4. Remove from heat. Allow to stand covered for several minutes before serving.

 ## East India Curry Dish

Serves 4

2 tablespoons safflower oil
1 onion, chopped
4 cloves garlic, minced
1 tablespoon curry powder
1 (10-ounce) can light coconut milk
1 head cauliflower, broken into small pieces
1 (16-ounce) can chickpeas, drained and rinsed
Salt to taste

1. In a large, heavy skillet heat the oil over high heat and add the onion and garlic, cooking until soft, about 5–6 minutes. Reduce the heat and add the curry powder, stirring well to roast the curry and coat the onions and garlic. *(continued)*

2. Cook another 3 minutes; then add the coconut milk, stirring well. Add the cauliflower and chickpeas.
3. Turn up the heat to medium until the milk begins to simmer. Reduce the heat, and simmer until the cauliflower is tender.
4. Serve over white or brown rice and top with roasted cashews or almonds.

Thursday

Upon rising: Lemon juice, water, and Stevia

Breakfast: Choice of a smoothie from Chapter 7, Coffee, Tea, and Chai Smoothies

Snack: 2 slices sprouted whole-grain bread with almond butter

Lunch: Roasted root vegetables tossed with balsamic vinaigrette; fish, chicken, or vegetarian protein; mixed green salad

Snack: Choice of a smoothie from Chapter 3, Smoothies for Fun

Dinner: Sautéed broccoli rabe with garlic on a whole-grain pizza crust, topped with pine nuts and Parmesan cheese (Try using soy Parmesan as an alternative.)

Friday

Upon rising: 1 teaspoon raw, unfiltered apple cider vinegar and 1 teaspoon raw honey in 8 ounces of water

Breakfast: Breakfast Grains

Snack: 1 apple, sliced and spread with almond butter

Lunch: Choice of a smoothie from Chapter 6, Low-Carb Smoothies

Snack: Mixed green salad with hummus and organic corn chips

Dinner: Vegetable Stir-Fry with nonwheat pasta

 Breakfast Grains

Serves 4

½ cup brown rice
½ cup whole spelt
¼ cup raisins

¼ cup sunflower seeds
½ teaspoon cinnamon
3 cups pure water

1. Before going to bed in the evening, combine the ingredients in a small slow cooker, cover, turn on low, and allow to cook until morning.
2. If not using a slow cooker, combine the ingredients in a medium-size saucepan, cover and soak overnight. In the morning, bring to a boil, reduce the heat to low, and simmer until all water is absorbed, about 30–40 minutes.
3. Serve with your choice of flax oil or butter, maple syrup or Stevia, milk or yogurt.

Saturday

Upon rising: Lemon juice, water, and Stevia

Breakfast: Bowl of fresh fruit topped with granola and yogurt

Snack: Glass of fresh organic vegetable juice

Lunch: Down Mexico Way 🥘, served with salsa, corn chips, and a green salad

Snack: Raw carrot, celery, and bok choy sticks

Dinner: Grilled fish, lightly cooked vegetables, and green salad

🍳 Down Mexico Way

Serves 4

1 tablespoon olive oil
1 medium onion, chopped
2 cloves garlic, minced
1 jalapeño pepper, minced (optional)
1 teaspoon ground cumin
1 (16-ounce) can black beans, drained and rinsed
Salt to taste
4 flour or corn tortillas, warmed
1 cup cooked brown rice
½ cup grated cheddar cheese
1 ripe avocado, pitted and sliced

1. In a heavy skillet, heat the oil and sauté the onion, garlic, and jalapeño until tender.
2. Add the cumin and stir well, cooking another 3–4 minutes. Add the black beans and salt and stir to combine.
3. On each tortilla, layer the rice, beans, cheese, and avocado; then roll tight.

Sunday

Upon rising: 1 teaspoon raw apple cider vinegar and 1 teaspoon raw honey in 8 ounces pure water

Brunch: Sunday Morning Happy Blues 🍳, served with maple syrup and organic butter

Snack: Choice of a smoothie from Chapter 2, Smoothies for Health

Dinner: Grilled vegetables, green salad, and vegetarian burgers with the works

Sunday Morning Happy Blues

Makes 8 pancakes

½ cup buttermilk
1 egg
2 tablespoons apple juice concentrate or honey
1 tablespoon safflower oil
1 teaspoon vanilla
½ cup whole wheat or spelt flour
1 teaspoon baking powder (nonaluminum brand)
1 cup fresh or frozen blueberries
real maple syrup

1. In a medium-size bowl, combine the first five ingredients, mixing well.
2. In a small bowl, combine the flour and baking powder.
3. Slowly add the flour mixture to the liquid ingredients, mixing well. Add the blueberries and mix gently.
4. Heat a heavy skillet over medium-high heat and spray lightly with a vegetable spray.
5. Pour ¼ cup of batter onto the hot skillet and cook until brown on 1 side, flip over, and brown the other side. Serve with real maple syrup.

The Low-Carb Week

In this seven-day menu plan, you will need to eliminate the following high-carbohydrate foods while limiting the use of others: Bread, cakes, cookies, refined grains, potatoes, sugar, honey, maple syrup, molasses, rice syrup, and barley malt. Your diet will be made up of 40 percent carbohydrates in the form of fresh vegetables and some fruits, 30 percent protein, and 30 percent good fats. Protein can be from vegetarian or animal sources, and smoothie recipes can be found in both Chapter 4, Low-Carb Smoothies, and Chapter 2, Smoothies for Health.

- Simplify your breakfast by having a smoothie with added fiber and protein powder, or eggs with vegetables.
- Make lunch your main meal of the day and have 4 ounces of animal protein with vegetables and salad.
- Make your dinner a vegetarian meal consisting of soup, salad, cooked vegetables, and protein from either tofu, tempeh, beans, or legumes.
- Have 2 tablespoons of good oils high in omega-3 fatty acids, such as flax seed, hemp, or borage oil.
- Use roasted nuts and seeds for snacks or with meals. When eating almonds or seeds raw, soak them in water for eight hours first, then drain and serve. This helps to make them more digestible for the body.
- Gradually ease yourself off fully caffeinated coffee by adding decaffeinated coffee each day until you are fully decaffeinated. Choose Swiss water–decaffeinated coffee that has been processed without chemicals.
- Explore the wide variety of coffee substitutes available on your local health food store shelves.
- Eat a variety of vegetables, but include green

vegetables such as kale, spinach, collards, arugula, watercress, broccoli, Swiss chard, escarole, bok choy, and Chinese cabbage on a daily basis.

- Instead of cooking with oil, try adding extra virgin olive oil or flax seed or hemp seed oil after the vegetables have been cooked in a small amount of water.
- Spray the cooking pan with oil to ensure that you use a small amount for cooking purposes.

Monday

Upon rising: Fresh lemon juice, water, and Stevia
Breakfast: Choice of a smoothie from Chapter 6, Low-Carb Smoothies
Snack: Baked tofu and roasted almonds
Lunch: Mixed green salad with grilled chicken, fish, or tempeh
Snack: Fresh berries in season
Dinner: Vegetarian Blue Ribbon Chili 🍲, bok choy stems with almond butter

Muffins

Low-carbohydrate ingredients are now available in most grocery and health food stores for making muffins and breads to use with this eating plan. Follow the package instructions to obtain the best results.

Vegetarian Blue Ribbon Chili

8 servings

Olive oil for cooking
1 medium onion, chopped
3 cloves garlic, minced
1 small green pepper, chopped
1 medium red pepper, chopped
2 teaspoons ground cumin
2 teaspoons ground cayenne
1 teaspoon dried ginger
1 teaspoon dried basil
1 teaspoon dried oregano
1 (28-ounce) can crushed organic tomatoes
1 (16-ounce) can diced tomatoes
Pinch of cinnamon
1 (16-ounce) can kidney beans, drained and rinsed
1 cup frozen corn
1 (16-ounce) can pitted black olives, diced
8 ounces soy or turkey sausage, chopped (optional)
Salt to taste

1. Spray the bottom of a large saucepan with olive oil and heat over medium-high heat. Add the onion, garlic, and peppers, stirring well. Add the cumin, cayenne, ginger, basil, and oregano, continuing to stir well for 2 minutes.
2. Add the remaining ingredients, salt to taste, reduce the heat, and simmer for 30 minutes, stirring occasionally.

Tuesday

Upon rising: Unsweetened cranberry juice with Stevia and water

Breakfast: Vegetable omelet with Avocado Salsa 🍳 and endive

Snack: 1 apple

Lunch: Vegetable Miso Soup 🍳

Snack: Choice of a smoothie from Chapter 2

Dinner: Quinoa Stir-Fry 🍳

🍳 Avocado Salsa

2 cups

1 (16-ounce) can diced tomatoes with basil
1 ripe avocado, peeled, pitted, and cubed
2 tablespoons fresh cilantro, diced
1 clove garlic, minced
Salt to taste

1. In a medium bowl, combine the ingredients and mix well.
2. Using a potato masher, press into the mixture several times to break apart the avocado. Don't overdo the mashing process. Serve on top of the omelet or scooped up with endive spears.

🍳 Vegetable Miso Soup

Serves 4

2 cups pure water
2 cups vegetable broth
1 medium carrot, chopped
4 shiitake mushrooms, stems removed, chopped

(continued)

4 teaspoons country barley miso
1 cup cooked kale, chopped
8 ounces grilled or poached fish, optional
Toasted pumpkin seeds for garnish

1. In a large saucepan combine the water, broth, carrot, and mushrooms over high heat. Bring to a boil, reduce heat, and simmer for 15 minutes.
2. When the carrots are tender and the mushrooms are cooked, turn off the heat and remove ⅓ cup liquid to a small bowl.
3. Dissolve the miso in the bowl of liquid and return to the pot of soup. Add the kale and allow to heat through.
4. Ladle into 4 soup bowls and divide the fish among the bowls. Top with toasted pumpkin seeds and serve immediately.

Quinoa Stir-Fry

Serves 4

1 cup quinoa
2 cups water
½ teaspoon sea salt
1 teaspoon extra virgin olive oil
1 medium leek, washed and chopped
2 cloves garlic, minced
2 medium carrots, julienned
6 baby zucchini, cut into half-moon slices
Salt to taste
1 teaspoon dried tarragon
1 (16-ounce) can white navy beans, drained
    and rinsed

(continued)

1. Rinse the quinoa in a mesh strainer under clean water. Drain and combine with 2 cups pure water and salt in a medium saucepan.
2. Bring to a boil, reduce heat, and simmer until water is absorbed, about 20 minutes.
3. Meanwhile, in a large, heavy skillet, heat the oil and sauté the leek and garlic until tender. Add the carrots and cook for 6 minutes, stirring well. Add the zucchini, salt, and tarragon. Stir, cover, and cook another 5 minutes.
4. Add the navy beans, stir, cover and cook until vegetables are just tender.
5. Spoon the quinoa into the center of each plate and top with the vegetables and beans.

Quinoa

Quinoa is a grain from the Andes that is high in protein, quick to cook, and can be served as a side dish or in a grain salad.

Wednesday

Upon rising: 1 teaspoon raw apple cider vinegar and Stevia in 8 ounces of water

Breakfast: Bowl of fresh berries with yogurt and walnuts

Snack: Choice of a smoothie from Chapter 6, Low-Carb Smoothies

Lunch: Chicken or vegetable stir-fry with green salad

Snack: Low-carb bread slice with almond butter

Dinner: Three Bean Salad 🍲 with grilled vegetables

Three Bean Salad
Serves 4

1 (16-ounce) can chickpeas, drained and rinsed
1 (16-ounce) can kidney beans, drained and rinsed
1 (16-ounce) can Great Northern beans, drained and rinsed
½ red onion, minced
1 cup corn kernels, cooked
1 cup arugula, chopped
2 tablespoons extra virgin olive or flax seed oil
3 tablespoons unrefined apple cider vinegar
Salt to taste

In a medium-size bowl, combine the ingredients and mix well. Cover and refrigerate for 1 hour for best results, but it can be served immediately if necessary.

Thursday
Upon rising: Lemon juice, water, and Stevia
Breakfast: Choice of a smoothie from Chapter 7, Coffee, Tea, and Chai Smoothies
Snack: 1 pear
Lunch: Baked Almond Fish and steamed vegetables
Snack: Choice of a smoothie from Chapter 6
Dinner: Stir-fried tempeh and vegetables

Baked Almond Fish
Serves 2

1 cup raw almonds
½ teaspoon sea salt
2 (4-ounce) white fish fillets, such as grouper
*   or tilapia oil*   (continued)

1. Preheat the oven to 375°F.
2. Place the almonds in a food processor and grind fine. Pour onto a plate and mix in the sea salt, being sure to spread the mixture out.
3. Wash and dry the fish; then, 1 at a time, press each fillet into the ground almonds.
4. Spray a baking dish with vegetable spray and place the fish fillets into the dish.
5. Spray the top of the fish lightly with oil and bake for 15–20 minutes, until the almonds have browned and the fish flakes when pierced with a fork.

Friday

Upon rising: Unsweetened cranberry juice, Stevia, and water
Breakfast: Choice of a smoothie from Chapter 6, Low-Carb Smoothies
Snack: Low-carb muffin
Lunch: Grilled salmon on a bed of steamed kale
Snack: Mixed green salad with toasted pine nuts
Dinner: Shrimp and Veggie Kabobs

Shrimp and Veggie Kabobs
Serves 4

1 medium onion
2 medium zucchini
1 red pepper
1 pound fresh shrimp, peeled and deveined
⅓ cup soy sauce
2 tablespoons rice wine (mirin)
1 tablespoon fresh lemon juice   *(continued)*

1. Prepare and heat the grill.
2. Chop the vegetables wide and thick enough to hold up to having a skewer stuck through the center of each piece.
3. Alternating ingredients, place on individual skewers, beginning with a piece of shrimp, then onion, zucchini, and red pepper. Repeat if there is room.
4. In a small bowl combine the soy sauce, rice wine, and lemon juice, and brush this mixture over the kabobs before and during the grilling process.

Saturday

Upon rising: 1 teaspoon raw apple cider vinegar and Stevia in 8 ounces water
Breakfast: Choice of a smoothie from Chapter 2, Smoothies for Health
Snack: 2 hard-boiled eggs
Lunch: Chicken salad on a bed of greens
Snack: 1 orange
Dinner: Grilled tempeh on a bed of watercress and arugula

Sunday

Upon rising: Lemon juice, water, and Stevia
Brunch: Lo-Carb Pancakes 🖙 with strawberries and yogurt
Snack: Baked tofu sandwich spread with almond or sesame butter
Dinner: Grilled fish and vegetables tossed with pesto sauce

Lo-Carb Pancakes
Makes 8–10 pancakes

1 cup ground flax seed meal   *½ teaspoon cinnamon*
⅓ cup walnuts, ground   *Stevia to taste*
1 teaspoon baking powder   *1 egg, beaten*
2 tablespoons yogurt   *1 teaspoon vanilla*
¾ cup water

1. Combine ingredients in a medium-size bowl, stirring well.
2. Heat a heavy skillet over medium-high, after having rubbed the bottom with salt. Spray with oil.
3. Ladle the pancake mixture into the skillet, forming 1 pancake at a time. Brown on 1 side before turning and cooking the other side.

No-Stick Pans

When not using Teflon-coated pans, and to prevent the first few pancakes from sticking, rub the bottom of the pan with a tablespoon of salt before heating Gently brush off the salt, spray with oil, and heat.

The Cleansing Week

Modern scientific research has shown in experiments that mice whose weight was kept low through a restriction of foods lived longer and more active lives than the mice who were allowed to grow fat from overeating. The point being, we don't need to consume as much food as we tend to eat, particularly since we have become a sedentary group of people. Reducing the amount of food over a period of time, then either eating a mono diet, consisting of one food, such as grapes for a day, or fasting on fresh juice and water, are all cleansing disciplines—mentioned seventy-four times in the Bible as a way to awaken and focus our spiritual lives. It also allows the digestive system to rest so that it can cleanse and restore the body after a long winter of heavy foods or holidays filled with sweets and fatty meals.

Proponents for periodic fasting claim that it slows down the aging process as the body reclaims its lost youthfulness and vitality. However, you will need to take the time to plan for your fast by setting aside a weekend when you won't be disrupted with work or strenuous activity, and then following the Healthy Balance and Low-Carb weeks in preparation for your cleansing. Consider this a special time for just yourself and the care of your body. Rest, read a good book, stay home and do beauty treatments for your skin and hair. Have a massage or reflexology treatment to stimulate the drainage of toxins from the body. Try to avoid negative people, movies, or television programs. Keep a journal during this time, writing down how you have been feeling, making goals for yourself, and looking at what stress-causing situations need to be eliminated from your life.

Cleansing is a simple eating plan that helps to rid the body of excess weight, toxins, and old fat. If you are interested in following the plan for a longer period of time, be sure to do so under the supervision of a medical expert.

As you follow this program, you will experience renewed vitality once your body is free of all that unnecessary bloat. Notice how the luster will be returned to your skin, the whites of your eyes will grow whiter, and your eyes will be clearer and sharper. This is the result of cleaning your major filtering organs, especially the liver, which can now do its many varied tasks with renewed efficiency. To maintain this transition toward optimal health, return to either the Healthy Balance Week or the Low-Carb Week and enjoy the feeling of living at your peak energy.

The Cleansing Week is a seven-day plan to prepare you for a weekend juice fast and to bring you back into eating a balanced diet. Here are suggestions to help you.

- It is best to ease into a fast by slowly modifying your diet so that you are ready to eliminate solid foods completely.
- Overeating the night before a fast will do more harm than good and will stretch out your stomach, making you more hungry than you would be otherwise. It will also cause you to have a sharp blood sugar dip the next day that will have you reaching for the first piece of food you can get your hands on.
- Follow the program and watch that bloated feeling disappear, restoring you to a calm, peaceful frame of mind.
- Begin the program on a Wednesday, allowing you three days to prepare your body, two days of fasting, and two days to come off the fast.

Each morning begin your day with freshly squeezed lemon juice, water, and Stevia.

Wednesday–Friday, Days 1–3

Breakfast: Choice of a smoothie from Chapter 2, Smoothies for Health, or Chapter 5, Healing Smoothies

Snack: Small bowl of cooked nongluten grain such as quinoa, brown rice, millet, buckwheat, or amaranth (follow package for cooking directions)

Snack: 1 piece of fresh fruit or fresh-squeezed vegetable juice

Lunch: Mixed green and raw vegetable salad with lemon, garlic, and extra virgin olive oil

Snack: Choice of a smoothie from Chapter 5, Healing Smoothies, or Homemade Vegetable Broth

Dinner: Steamed vegetables with Lemon Garlic Dressing

Homemade Vegetable Broth

Serves 4

1 medium onion, chopped
3 cloves garlic, sliced
2 stalks celery, chopped
1 carrot, chopped
2 unpeeled potatoes, chopped

Choice of handful of
  greens: kale,
  collards, dandelion,
  watercress
8 cups of pure water

Combine ingredients and simmer.

Salty Broths

Store-bought vegetable broth can contain high amounts of salt. You can make your own delicious broth by simmering the vegetables mentioned in a large saucepan with 8 cups of pure water, cooling when done, and storing in the refrigerator.

Lemon Garlic Dressing
Makes ½ cup of dressing

> *Juice of 2 lemons*
> *½ cup organic extra virgin olive oil*
> *2 cloves garlic, minced or pressed*

Combine in a small jar and shake well before using.

Weekend Fast

Make your last meal an early Friday dinner. Eat lightly, chew your foods well, and go to bed at a reasonable hour. Begin your fast on Saturday morning with a cup of lemon water, breaking the fast on Monday morning with fresh fruit.

Breakfast: Cup of herbal tea such as kukicha (roasted twig tea), dandelion, nettle, or mint
Midmorning: 4 ounces fresh vegetable juice such as carrot, ginger, and parsley diluted with 4 ounces of pure distilled water (see the "Vegetable Juice Combinations" section in Chapter 5, Healing Smoothies)
Midafternoon: 1 cup herbal tea or warm vegetable broth
Evening: 4 ounces vegetable juice diluted with pure distilled water
Before bedtime: Fresh lemon juice with distilled water

Breaking the Fast

End your fast on Monday morning with your lemon juice and water. You will need to limit the amount of food you have on this first day back eating solid food. Your stomach and intestines have contracted and won't be able to handle large amounts of food.

Breakfast: 8 ounces of a smoothie from Chapter 2, Smoothies for Health, or Chapter 5, Healing Smoothies
Lunch: Raw vegetable salad consisting of grated carrots, beets, cabbage, and finely chopped celery tossed with lemon juice
Dinner: Steamed vegetables with Lemon Garlic Dressing and Homemade Vegetable Broth

Day Seven
Upon rising: Juice of ½ lemon in water
Breakfast: 8 ounces of a smoothie from Chapter 2 or Chapter 5 with 1 tablespoon flax seed meal
Snack: Piece of fresh fruit
Lunch: Raw salad with lemon, extra virgin olive oil, and garlic, brown rice with 1 tablespoon flax seed meal
Snack: Choice of a smoothie from Chapter 5
Dinner: Vegetable soup, salad, and sprouted grain bread

Resume eating your normal healthy diet on Day Eight.

All along the journey toward better health, you can use your copy of *Simply Smoothies* to help with new and creative ideas when planning a quick meal or snack. Share what you learn with family and friends and watch their health improve as well—it is the greatest gift you can give and the one they will appreciate for years to come.

Conclusion
As you can see, there are enough smoothie recipes to keep your blender busy for a long time. Smoothies are a

great morning jump-start; a quick meal to refresh your mind, body, and spirit after a long day; and the perfect way to perk up a party or get-together. That's the beauty of this book—smoothies are America's new favorite drink, and they are versatile enough to complement any situation.

For hectic days when a breakfast on the run is all you have time for, smoothies are the perfect grab-and-go meal. For that midafternoon energy slump, smoothies can provide a nutritious boost. For the times you crave a rich, sweet dessert, you can always turn to Chapter 3, Smoothies for Fun, to satisfy that sweet tooth.

When trying to ward off a cold, boost your immune system, or maintain a balanced level of energy, you can always turn to Chapter 2, Smoothies for Health, and Chapter 5, Healing Smoothies, to keep you on track. And last but not least, the recipes in Chapter 8, Party Smoothies, are the perfect way to enjoy the little things in life with friends and family. With or without alcohol, these fun recipes are perfect for just about any occasion.

Never before has a single drink changed the way we look at food, health, and life. Remember, when making your smoothies, experimenting is half the fun! Don't be afraid to try different ingredients and substitutions to make your own customized smoothie recipes. The Smoothie Ingredients Chart (page 196) provides easy reference for creative combinations of your favorite ingredients, with endless possibilities. Here you can let your creative juices flow, and with *Simply Smoothies* as your guide, create hundreds of refreshing drinks for years to come.

Smoothie Ingredients Chart

Fruits
bananas
coconuts
strawberries
blueberries
raspberries
blackberries
cranberries
grapes
avocados
peaches
mangoes
papayas
cherries
apricots
plums
lemons
limes
oranges
grapefruits
pomegranates
watermelons
apples
pears
melons
dates
raisins
currants
figs
apricots

Fruits/Vegetables
tomatoes
cucumbers
peppers

Liquids
pineapple
blueberry
apple
orange
orange/carrot
raspberry
grape
coconut
mango
papaya
piña colada
Vruit
prune
cherry
pomegranate
mixed vegetable
guava
soy
rice
oat
almond
soy/rice
organic milk
goat's milk
purified water
yogurt
soy yogurt
silken tofu
chai tea
green tea
filtered ice

Extras
soy
rice
whey
Ultimate Meal
flax seed meal
flax seed oil
walnuts
cinnamon
vanilla
almond extract
maple extract
hazelnut extract
almonds
sesame seeds
honey
maple syrup
Stevia
Sucanat
juice concentrates

Index